JOE

JOE

THE COFFEE BOOK

Jonathan and Gabrielle Rubinstein and Company

with Judith Choate

PHOTOGRAPHY BY STEVE POOL

Lyons Press is an imprint of Globe Pequot Press.

Project editor: David Legere
Text design: Jason Snyder
Layout artist: Nancy Freeborn

Photographs in Chapter 1 by Amanda Byron, with the exception of cup image on page 2 © Steve Pool and branch image on page 9 licensed by Shutterstock.com. All other images © Steve Pool.

Library of Congress Cataloging-in-Publication Data is available on file.

ISBN 978-0-7627-7865-2

Printed in China
10 9 8 7 6 5 4 3 2 1

To all our "Joeys," past and present—our amazing crew of baristas, BITs, managers, trainers, barbacks, and "above" folk—who present our coffees in a way that makes us proud, every day.

E N T S

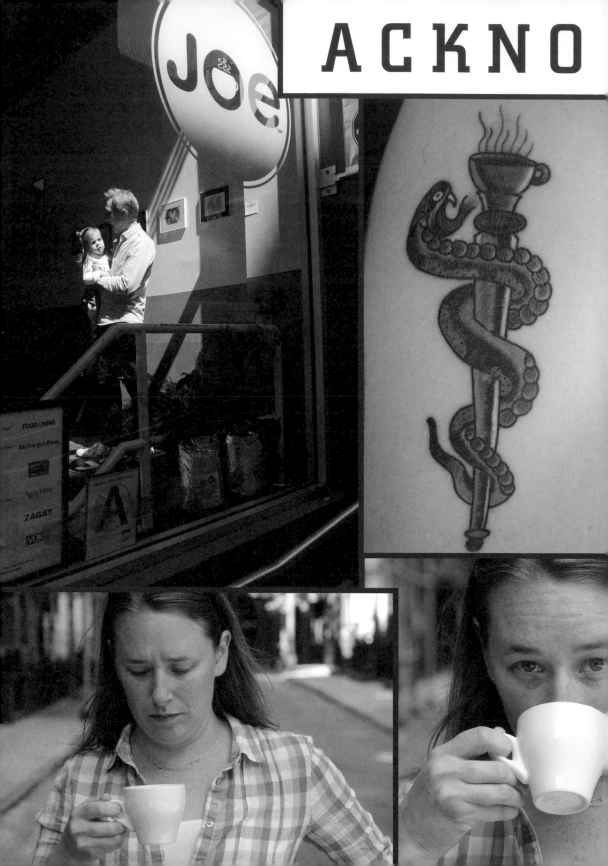

WLEDGMENTS

There are so many people who have been instrumental in making this book happen.

First and foremost, our Vice President and Director of Coffee, our first employee, the "Other" author of this book, and the "Other Rubinstein," Amanda Byron. She is the great unsung hero of **joe**, the voice of reason, a woman of vision, and the one who constantly brings us back to our mission of great coffee.

Thanks to our parents, Richard and Alice Rubinstein, without whom **joe** wouldn't exist. They give us roots and wings every day and allow us to steer the ship as we see fit.

Thanks to our friends at Ecco Caffè, most specifically Andrew Barnett, Doug Zell, Amber Fox, David Latourell, Steve Mierisch, and Ramin Narimani for taking such great care of us and for all your help and guidance with the text.

Thanks to Michael and Ben and First Press for helping to make people aware of what we do.

Thanks to Barth and Gregg and everyone at Barrington Coffee—our first partners and a constant source of inspiration. Thanks to Mary Norris and David Legere of Lyons Press as well as Grainne Fox and Christy Fletcher—our supportive and hard working team of editors and agents who made this beautiful book a reality. And thanks to Steve Poole and Judith Choate for coming up with the idea of this book . . . and for more than just a wee bit of the work in making it happen.

Most importantly, to our amazing group of managers, educators, and baristas, who serve our coffee to the people . . . there are too many of you to name individually, but we are blessed to have your culinary skill, and your warmth and integrity. Thank you for making us and our customers happy, one cup at a time.

How many times have you heard someone say, "I'd like a nice, hot cup of coffee!"? (I know, I know, it really should be a nice cup of hot coffee, but nobody ever says that!) In our family, it was my mom, Alice, who was forever on the quest, not for a nice cup of hot coffee but for the perfectly made latte. For years, she was obsessive, going from coffee shop to coffeehouse to bistro to trattoria scouting out that elusive cup. She'd order, sip, grimace, and move on. Mom's infatuation became a family joke, but we were so often on the trail together that her passion lured the rest of us deep into latte-land. We all joined in the chase for the perfect cup.

What had been our in-house gag turned into a serious venture when I found myself (joyfully) unemployed and thinking about changing careers.

The SEARCH for the SOUL of a GREAT CUP of COFFEE

I had always been fascinated with food and the world of hospitality, but I had no interest in cooking or opening a restaurant. Besides, New York City, my home, had an excess of world-renowned dining and drinking establishments, and frankly, I didn't think that I knew enough about the restaurant business to make an impact in this mecca of all things culinary. But, interestingly, back in 2002 New York City didn't have one great coffee bar, a place where people could socialize, ponder, read, advocate for change, or just sit back and relax, all the while enjoying a matchless "cuppa joe." So, coffee moved to the top of my career-change list, and along with my sister, Gabrielle, and my parents, Alice and Richard, the hunt for the perfectly made latte became a search for a perfect coffee bar of our own.

Unfortunately, none of us knew much about how to accomplish our dream bar. We knew little about the when, where, and how of great coffee, except that we seemed inherently to know it when we tasted it. We did know a bit about real estate and had a clear idea about the kind of location and coffee bar we wanted. It was Gabrielle who made the first connection to the long line of serendipitous links that created our first **joe**.

Apprenticing as an opera singer at the Tanglewood Music Center in the Berkshire Hills of Massachusetts, Gabby discovered the elusive cup at Lenox Coffee, owned by a partner at Barrington Coffee Roasting Company in Great Barrington. Not only did

she find great coffee, but she also discovered the Barrington owners, Barth Anderson and Gregg Charbonneau. They stood right on the cutting edge of the third wave of coffee, using select beans and roasting them in-house. At Gabby's urging, we made the trip to the Berkshires, not to hear her sing, but to sip, sip, sip. Barth and Gregg became our mentors, introducing us to some of the history of coffee, the necessities of a great cup, and the people who would help us bring our own style of coffee bar to blasé New Yorkers. In fact, they led us to Amanda Byron, our first employee, who had worked at their roastery. Amanda is still with us and has gone on to become vice president of our

company and director of coffee for all of the **joe** stores.

We chose Greenwich Village for our first location, mainly because of its coffeehouse history. The area had traditionally been the landmark for bohemian life in America, with new ideas, political movements, and artistic chaos emanating from its cafés, homes, and streets. Historically, the Village had been the home of writers, artists, and thinkers who gathered in the many dark, smoky coffeehouses that were the signature watering holes of the area from the early 1900s through the 1960s. Not only did art and culture thrive in the liberal atmosphere of the neighborhood coffee

café, but in the late 1950s, the off-Broadway theater was born at Caffè Cino, one of the most enlightened coffeehouses of the era. Although bohemian life in the Village has given way to expensive real estate, the coffeehouse culture has prevailed, and we could think of no other area of the city in which a new style coffee bar could thrive.

In 2003, we opened our "utopian" coffee bar at the intersection of Waverly Place and Gay Street, a magical corner on a street bathed in the light of an esteemed past. In the 1800s Gay Street was home to many of the African-American servants who were employed by the rich and famous Washington Square families well documented by Edith Wharton and Henry James. In the early 1900s, artists and writers were attracted to its inexpensive rents and charming meandering cobblestones. The charm had lasted, and we felt that this unique area would welcome a return to its coffeehouse past with a new twist—an incomparable cup of coffee made with concerns for contemporary political, social, and environmental health. A visionary dream, perhaps, but one we felt we could realize.

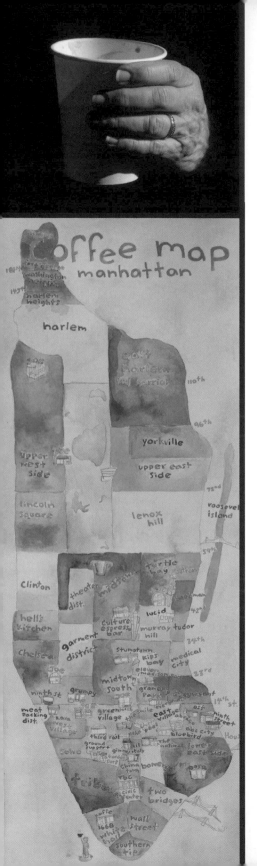

coffee map
manhattan

The world of artisanal coffee had long been established in the western United States with Seattle (including Starbucks, which set the international trend), Portland, and San Francisco the leading lights in the development of the interaction between farmer, importer, roaster, coffee bar, and customer. In an attempt to catch up with the West, we hired the few trained coffee mavens we could find, purchased the best equipment available, used beans from Barrington Coffee Roasting Company, tested cup upon cup, and read as many books as were available on the subject of coffee. Unlike many other "coffeehouses," we set out to do one thing well—create a focused coffee bar, treating coffee as a serious culinary art.

Although we had defined the product we wanted to sell, we had absolutely no idea how the availability of great coffee would quickly and drastically move forward. The changing social awareness at the start of the twenty-first century brought a new mission to the coffee market. Fair Trade commerce led to Direct Trade (see page 13); the skill of a trained barista became a marketable quality, and a desirable career was born for many focused young people; the knowledge and sophistication of coffee drinkers grew exponentially; and with all of this, the demand for the perfect cup of coffee grew faster than we could have imagined when we brought our idea to realization.

When **joe** opened in 2003, there were just a few trained baristas working in New York

City, and most consumers demanded nothing more than a hot beverage served in the ubiquitous paper cup covered with traditional Greek Anthora design. Much has changed in the world of artisanal coffee in the brief period that has passed since then. The coffee "scene" has switched to New York, with some of the western coffee bars, such as San Francisco's Blue Bottle Coffee, gaining a foothold in the city along with quite a number of New York originals, like Café Grumpy and Gimme! Coffee, setting the pace. And, with the recent news that a major investment firm has purchased a controlling interest in Stumptown, one of New York's premier specialty coffee bars, the tide has turned from entrepreneurial excitement to big business. This makes it ever more important for us, at **joe,** to stay ahead of the coffee curve, keeping our goals and focus the same as always. We like to think that we are, as we keep the spotlight on ethically grown and processed beans, beginning a program to connect our employees with coffee farmers, sponsor a training center for baristas, compost and recycle most of the waste in our stores, advocate for social equity, lead classes open to the public to develop an understanding of the soul of a great cup of coffee, and even organize our own noncompetitive but fun **joe** running team. And with this, **joe** has expanded to a group of coffee bars in New York City with loyal consumers constantly asking us to bring the **joe** experience to their little corner of the city.

In a short period of time, we have seen coffee go from its first wave, when it was viewed simply as a commodity to be processed and canned for supermarket distribution to the second wave, initiated in Berkeley, California, in the late 1960s by Alfred Peet at Peet's Coffee and Tea, with its focus on roasting and serving a number of varietals and signature coffees (and teas). Peet's inspired the founding and growth of Seattle-based Starbucks, which made coffee awareness a national and an international phenomenon with the spotlight on espresso drinks and single origin coffees. This enormous expansion brought about the current movement, or third wave, whereby the focal point is on viewing coffee as an artisanal foodstuff, like wine. This

entails the production of premium coffees on carefully managed farms, the selection and roasting of the beans by skilled artisans, and the creation of signature blends and specialty coffees by trained baristas using the most proficient equipment.

Although making great coffee has been and will remain the focus at **joe,** as a family run business, it is important to all of us that we are ethical and involved in the community—both the international coffee community and our immediate neighborhood—and that each of our stores is a nurturing environment for our employees and our customers. We try to operate our coffee world much as we run our personal lives, and as such, we have found that we are happy to come to work, our baristas thrive, and our customers get the ultimate coffee experience in welcome and warmth. We like to say that **joe** hospitality has to match the quality of **joe** coffee. We hope that you will drop in and experience a little of both.

Jonathan Rubinstein

SPILLING the BEANS

SPILLING the BEANS

When we began our quest for the finest cup of coffee that we could produce, we had no idea that we would need to immerse ourselves in the story of coffee—the history, agriculture, and politics of its growth. But, to understand the core of the cup, we found that we did need to have a basic comprehension of the where and why of the bean—particularly since we wanted to tie the product we would be selling to our social consciousness.

As a major agricultural export for many impoverished (and now developing) countries, coffee has historically been traded on the backs of the poor and disenfranchised. Colonial powers blossomed through the enslavement of native workers throughout Indonesia, Africa, and Latin America. Coffee has not had a pretty history. So, although this history has created the future, our interest is in the more recent fair and equitable turn that specialty coffee trading has taken.

Like many foods with a long history, coffee comes with varied and somewhat questionable tales of its origin and many myths associated with its global reach. However, one fact seems clear: coffee is indigenous to Ethiopia. It is believed that its name comes, in part, from the particular area of the country, Kaffa, where it is native as well as from *kafa,* the Ethiopian word for it. The most oft-told tale is that its energizing effects were first discovered in the mid-800s by an Ethiopian goatherd named Kaldi, who noticed that after eating the berries from local trees his goats danced and caroused in a lively fashion. He joined them in the feast and quickly found that he, too, could mimic their enthusiastic partying. Nearby monks took to the habit and turned the berries into a drink that helped them concentrate on their religious studies. With this mythical beginning coffee began its travels around

the world—first as a drink used in religious practices, then through broad medicinal use, and finally as a social drink firmly established throughout the Middle East.

Coffee consumption and culture were an integral part of daily life in Ethiopia long before its adaptation by other cultures. It wasn't until the 1600s that coffee began its move from the Muslim world and took its place in European societies as coffeehouses opened across the continent and the United Kingdom. Unlike almost everything else in "polite" society, coffeehouses were open to all classes of people, and this affected their acceptance as well as their prohibition. The energizing effect of the drink only heightened vigorous political and social intercourse, which, in turn, was often the seed of social unrest. So, while the ordinary man enjoyed the freedoms generated by the sociability of the drinking house, authorities frequently found coffeehouses to be the setting for seditious behavior and used various tactics to suppress them. However, over generations, coffee drinking and coffeehouses became so firmly entrenched throughout the world that, despite taxation, prohibition, royal decree, abolishment, and censorship, they persevered as the meeting place of choice for the general population. And, today, we are seeing select specialty coffee bars as both the meeting place and the magnet for socially conscious activists.

Although Ethiopia is the birthplace of coffee, coffee trees are now found in a number of regions between the Tropic of Cancer and the Tropic of Capricorn. In fact, almost all of the world's finest coffees come from three growing regions: East Africa/

Arabia, the Pacific/Indonesia, and the Americas. All of the coffee-producing countries in these regions share a commonality: a mountainous, subtropical climate and an equatorial position, both of which combine to produce superior coffee beans. Within these areas, specialty coffee is most often cultivated at higher altitudes, usually from 3,500 to 6,500 feet, because it is generally felt that the higher the altitude, the denser, more deeply flavored the harvested bean. No matter the area, coffee farming is a difficult, arduous, and financially challenging business.

To ensure that we fully understand the scope and intensity of the production of specialty coffees, we frequently send our leading baristas to the place of origin during harvest. During this indoctrination they observe exactly how quality beans go from tree to cup so that they can convey the depth of the specialty coffee program to **joe** customers. It is important that we all understand that coffee is much more than just a commodity to be consumed; it is the means of survival for vast numbers of marginal lives across the globe. During these visits, our baristas walk among the trees, tasting the ripe cherries, interacting with the farmers and pickers, and learning from the bottom up.

Although coffee trees can grow to great heights when left on their own, they are usually pruned to a manageable height when farmed. Usually no more than ten to twelve feet tall at their highest, the coffee trees or bushes are generally covered

COFFEE FACTS:

Coffee first appeared in the American colonies in 1670, advertised by a Dorothy Jones in Boston.

by larger shade-producing trees to protect them from intense, direct sunlight during the day and inclement weather at all times, particularly killing frosts. Additionally the shade cover provides an even temperature through the cooler evening hours, giving the trees steady warmth. Often the shade trees are fruit-producing, which also offers another source of income for the farmer. Almost all coffee trees are young, under twenty-five years old, to ensure vigorous output, as older trees lose much of their productivity.

As important as shade-grown coffee farming is, specialty coffees can also be grown in nonforested areas. These regions were originally grasslands with few shade trees in their landscape. For instance, Brazil's Cerrado (in the state of Minas Gerais) produces much-esteemed specialty coffees without the canopy of shade trees. As in life, it seems there is always an exception in coffee growing.

The shade-grown method of coffee farming is known as an agroforestry structure—the primary product, coffee, is treated as an underbrush to the shade cover, which is most often a combination of fruit trees, perennial large-leafed banana plants, and hardwood trees. This method provides protection from soil erosion, maintains favorable and stable temperature and humidity, replenishes the soil with rotting organic matter from the plants and trees, and offers a home to beneficial insects. In fact, this traditional approach to coffee farming is considered

COFFEE FACTS:

A typical coffee tree produces about one pound of coffee annually. It takes four to five years for a new tree to bear a usable crop of fruit.

one of the most ecologically anchored and environmentally favorable agro-ecosystems. Little did we know that by choosing specialty coffee, **joe** would be playing a part in sustainable agriculture.

Coffee is grown on a number of differing types of farms. The largest, worldwide, are estates also known as fincas (or *fazendas*), estancias, or plantations, depending upon the locale; they are usually a large landmass with multiple buildings and on site processing run by an individual or a family, sometimes an extended one. These operations generally offer very consistent supervision of the farming and the processing but also face devastation in years of bad weather or local upheavals when an entire expansive harvest can be lost. Coffees from estates will often offer high-quality, defined, and recognizable flavors in a roasted bean. However, there

exist privately owned estates that lack the care or craftsmanship required to properly prepare and sort their harvested cherries. The simple fact is that many estates produce coffee of superior quality while others do not. The next largest type would be farm-cooperatives, which are associations of farmers joined together in their common interest. The main drawback to the cooperative method of selling coffee is that an extremely desirable bean may be combined with inferior beans, resulting in less reward for the more passionate farmer who has produced it. There are a number of coffee cooperatives that are exemplary in sorting their coffee cherries and have a high degree of craftsmanship. A case in point is the Konga Cooperative in Ethiopia's Yirgacheffe region. Finally, there are the small farms owned by an individual or a family where the coffee can range from exceptional to ordinary. On these small farms, it is possible for roasters to work one on one with the grower to develop phenomenal coffees. However, in a continuing search for the best possible bean, the specialty coffee roaster works with all types of growers.

Almost every coffee-growing region has a single harvest each year, but there are exceptions. For instance, Colombia has two harvests, consisting of one main crop and another usually smaller one called *mitaca* or *traviesa* (fly-crop); however, the Santander, Boyaca, and Sierra Nevada Colombian coffees are only harvested once, during the second semester of the year. (The first semester begins in April and ends in July while the second begins in September and ends in December.)

In the specialty coffee market, the goal is to convey the dried beans to the roaster as quickly as possible so that the beans can be prepared for the consumer when the level of freshness and vibrancy is at its highest. Therefore, just as a buyer visits a farmers' market for of-the-moment produce, seasonality is perhaps the most potent selling point of an artisanal coffee. Again, there are a few exceptions, with the Monsooned Malabar and Aged Sumatra coffees rested and then aged for many months and sometimes years. At **joe,** as well as at other top specialty coffee bars, primarily seasonal coffees are served.

Currently, most specialty coffees come from growers in Nicaragua, Brazil, Bolivia, Colombia, Costa Rica, El Salvador, Guatemala, Ethiopia, Rwanda, Yemen, Honduras, India, Indonesia, Peru, Panama, Burundi, Tanzania, and Kenya. All of the estates, cooperatives, or farms support sustainable and, often, organic agricultural practices, with the farmers realizing maximum profit for their efforts through the Direct Trade system (see page 13). Through this system coffee roasters, such as Ecco/Intelligentsia, our current **joe** roasters, buy their green beans directly from the farm, eliminating the traditional buyers and giving the roasters firsthand knowledge of the farm's practices. This system is somewhat different from other socially conscious and certified methods such as Fair Trade (see page 17) because of the straight line from farm to cup, building strong, enduring relationships among all of the participants along that line. Ecco/Intelligentsia has even trademarked the certification Intelligentsia Direct Trade, which indicates the standards (including its relationship with farmers) set for its coffee. Other roasters generally have similar programs to give them greater control over the quality of the coffee and to make sure that

specific concerns about environmental and social issues are met. To the point, when purchasing green coffee, a fine quality roaster targeting ethical principles intends for the coffee farmer to receive the same international accolades and recognition as the proprietor of a vineyard would receive from the wine industry.

To this end, in the early 2000s a few dedicated specialty coffee buyers and roasters created a program called Cup of Excellence. The program was spearheaded by George Howell, a Boston-based pioneer in the specialty coffee business; Susie Spindler, an early promoter of artisanal coffees; and Silvio Leite, a Brazilian coffee expert. Funded by the International Coffee Organization, the International Trade Center, and the United Nations Common Fund for Commodities, the project grew out of the founders' frustration with the lack of appreciation for high-quality Brazilian coffees among North American specialty coffee buyers. It has grown to become an internationally known, strictly ruled yearly competition

that chooses the finest coffee produced in a country. A jury of international coffee experts selects the winning coffees, and the final stars of the crop are auctioned via the Internet to the highest bidder. Coffees deserving of the award are extremely rare; they must be perfectly ripe when picked and exhibit a well-developed body, a pleasant aroma, and a lively sweetness, qualities only found in carefully grown, exemplary coffees. As with wine, each Cup of Excellence winner manifests its own signature flavor redolent of the terroir in which it is grown and is managed throughout the growing and drying process in a manner that enhances its unique characteristics.

Through the Cup of Excellence program, an individual grower is shown the importance of quality in relation to price, as the auctioned coffee always enjoys a high premium. And, more importantly, the grower receives 85 percent of the auction price. This esteemed program advocates cooperation among every level of international specialty coffee production and sales and promotes alliances among individual growers in a country.

All specialty coffees, no matter their homeland, are *Coffea arabica,* the seed of a cherry-like fruit produced by a perennial evergreen tree. (There is another widely grown coffee, *Coffea canephora,* more commonly known as *Coffea robusta,* that not only produces far greater yields than *arabica* but is also resistant to disease. However, it is only used for large-scale commercial coffee production and is rarely found in specialty coffee). To produce a fine coffee, the cherries must be handpicked at the

11

perfect degree of ripeness, a labor-
intensive job. The landscape is fairly
rugged and uneven, the undergrowth
is thick, the cherries are of a differing
degree of ripeness on each branch, and,
as with most fruit trees, the fruit grows
randomly along the branches. The picker
tries to lift only those cherries that are
at the height of their ripeness, ruby red
and Bing cherry–like, although mistakes
are easily made and less ripe cherries
often make it into the picker's basket.
Both underripe and overripe cherries will
be sour, with the underripe also quite
astringent and the overripe tasting salty
and fermented—not desirable flavors
when creating a fine coffee. We have
visited farms during harvest and can
assure you that we came away with a deep
admiration for the farmers and workers

and clearly understood why premium coffee demands a premium price.

After picking, the cherries require extensive processing to get to a marketable
state. There is an ancient process now known as the natural/dry process whereby
the picked cherries are dried in the sun before processing begins. Drying takes
approximately two weeks, and the cherries are constantly raked to prevent mold from
forming on the moist fruit. When the cherries are completely dry, the outer skin,
pulp, and parchment are removed. Because this natural method requires a climate
that is normally extremely hot and arid, it is mostly done in Yemen, Ethiopia, and
areas of Brazil. However, since it is thought that the dry process yields coffees with
deeper, more rounded body and less acidity, a number of Central American producers
have been experimenting with producing natural/dry processed coffees. The Peterson
family of Panama's legendary Hacienda La Esmeralda and Aida Battle, owner of El
Salvador's award-winning Finca Kilimanjaro, have been branching out, processing

DIRECT TRADE

Direct Trade is a term used by coffee roasters who buy straight from the farmers, cutting out the traditional middleman buyers/sellers. We believe Direct Trade is the best model because it builds mutually beneficial and respectful relationships with individual farmers or cooperatives while paying the highest price for exceptional beans and demanding sustainable environmental and social practices.

CRITERIA:

> Coffee quality must be exceptional.

> The verifiable price to the grower or local co-op—not simply the exporter— must be at least 25 percent above the Certified Fair Trade price.

> The grower must be committed to healthy environmental practices.

> The grower must be committed to sustainable social practices.

> Ecco Caffè representatives must visit the farm or cooperative village at least once per harvest season.

> All participants must be open to transparent disclosures of financial deliveries back to the individual farmers.

COFFEE FACTS:

In the early 1700s London had more than two thousand coffeehouses.

COFFEE FACTS:

One hundred percent of all coffee is grown between the Tropic of Cancer and the Tropic of Capricorn. *Coffea arabica,* the finest bean grown, gets its name from the original promoters of great coffee, the Arabs, who in the fifteenth century brought it from East Africa to the Arabian Peninsula.

their coffees using this traditional method.

Perhaps one of the strangest, costliest, and most coveted of all coffees is *kopi luwak* or civet cat coffee. Found in the Philippines and Indonesia, it is created when coffee cherries are eaten by the civet cat, passed through the digestive tract, and then excreted, essentially as processed beans. The seeds are fermented by the stomach acids and enzymes, which supposedly gives the coffee brewed from them an incredibly smooth, velvety flavor with no bitterness on the palate. The beans are washed thoroughly, sun-dried, and very lightly roasted. Only *kopi luwak* found in

the wild is in demand, and it is quite rare. The retail cost per pound is two hundred to three hundred dollars.

In all other areas, once the cherries have been picked, they must be washed and sorted. As they make their way through water-filled canals, underripe cherries will rise to the top, and sorters will pick out diseased, damaged, or overripe cherries by hand. The next step is to squeeze the seed from the fruit, a system called depulping, which can be done by hand-operated machines on small farms or by large-scale machinery in larger processing plants.

After depulping, the seeds are still covered by a thin layer of mucilage, which must be removed. This can be done by one of three methods: pulped natural, aqua-pulping, or washed. The first method allows the beans to dry naturally in the sun, and with the second, the beans are machine-scrubbed to remove the covering. The third, whereby the beans are steeped in water to create fermentation, is the preferred method for specialty coffee beans as accurate fermentation ensures perfectly balanced body and fruit in the roasted bean. After fermentation, the seeds are washed to eliminate any lasting mucilage

FAIR TRADE LABELING:

Fair Trade is an organization that aims to help farmers in developing countries make better trading conditions and promotes sustainability. The movement advocates the payment of a higher price than the commodity market to farmers and to help improve their quality of life as well as their environmental standards in farming.

CRITERIA:

> The coffee was produced by a member of a democratically run cooperative.

> A minimum of $1.31 per pound of green, unroasted coffee was paid to the farmer for conventional coffee, and a minimum of $1.41 was paid for Certified Organic.

> The producers had access to preharvest credit.

> Certification was done by a recognized third-party authority (Transfair USA in the United States).

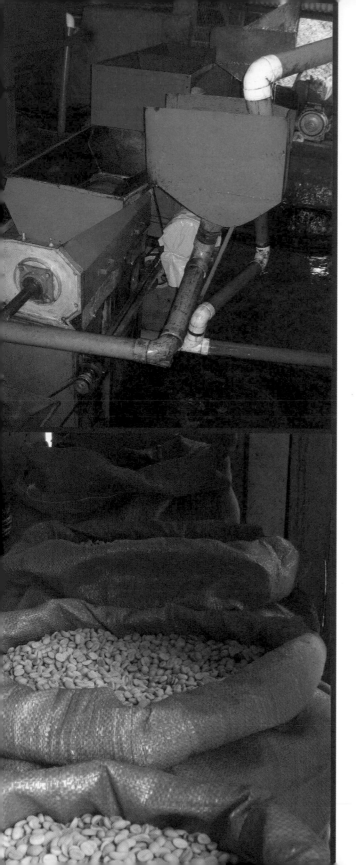

cover and are then laid out on concrete slabs or raised mesh screens to dry in the sun. All during the drying process, the beans are frequently raked over the slabs or tossed on the screens to generate uniform drying. They can also be mechanically dried by spinning them in rotating drums at a fairly constant low temperature.

As the seeds dry, a parchment-like film blooms. This serves to protect the drying coffee until it reaches the appropriate 12 percent level of humidity. If the beans do not reach the desired level of humidity, they can develop a variety of problems, such as mold, during shipping and will be unusable. Yet, when the beans are overdry, they may easily crack, and the finished flavor will be dull and woody with indistinct acidity, not desirable qualities at all.

To ensure quality flavor the dried beans must rest in their parchment covering. This dormant process can take thirty to sixty days. During this resting period, the humidity equalizes

BIRD FRIENDLY CERTIFICATION
(also Shade Grown)

Bird Friendly certification attests to the fact that the coffee farm has not cut down the trees and plant life that create the natural habitat for birds and the whole ecosystem. It is important to note that specialty level coffee is, by default, shade grown, because it requires a certain amount of shade throughout its growth to properly ripen.

CRITERIA:

> Certification is done through the Smithsonian Migratory Bird Center.

> The coffee is shade-grown in a forest-like habitat friendly to migrating and local birds.

> The coffee is grown on organic farms in Latin America.

> No chemical pesticides are allowed.

throughout the batch and the beans are rendered more resistant to breakage and damage from variations in humidity and external pressures. When beans are evaluated too early in the resting period, they often display grassy or vegetal characteristics that do not give a clear example of their final, fully rested state.

After rest, the remaining parchment-like covering must be removed. This is accomplished in a deparching/hulling machine. Then, again, the beans must be sorted, usually by machine, to give a final cleaning as well as to remove any remaining defects. Finally, the beans are hand-sorted to eliminate those that have undesirable color, are broken, or have any previously undetected blemishes. This final sorting is the most important as, with the proverbial one bad apple spoiling the barrel, a few bad beans can completely diminish the excellence of the cup.

Throughout the drying and cleaning process, the beans may or may not be tested for quality through "cupping," a standard method of quality control (see pages 30 and 38). Optimally, sample cuppings should be done at the farm with freshly harvested beans. In part, this allows the farmer to fully comprehend the flavor profiles desired by a specialty roaster. Unfortunately, this practice does not happen often. Generally the responsibility of tasting and qualifying is left to agronomists, buyers, or "cuppers" at a cooperative or processing source. However, in the last decade, due to the growth of the Direct Trade movement, we have seen a trend whereby the more progressive and quality-focused farms are instituting quality control programs on site. In addition, we have seen a growth in cooperation between farmers and green-bean buyers that involves them tasting their beans together. All of the discrimination that goes into selecting fine quality beans also goes into selecting and processing decaffeinated beans. In addition, the search continues for improved methods of removing the caffeine. Because of the time and effort involved in creating it, decaffeinated coffee carries a wholesale cost substantially higher than nondecaffeinated beans, but this cost is rarely reflected in its retail price. All of the decaffeinated coffee that we serve at **joe** has been carefully selected and decaffeinated through either the water process or the German/European (MC/methylene chloride) process. Both processes use the indirect method of decaffeinating whereby the activated agent does not come in direct contact with the coffee beans. The decaffeinating process known as the direct method is never used in the specialty coffee business.

During the decaffeinating process the green coffee beans are soaked in large tanks of water, which releases the caffeine from the pores of the beans. The soaking water is drained from the tank and treated with a chemical agent to extract the caffeine. Then the caffeine and the chemical are removed from the water, and the beans are reintroduced to the solution to drink in the flavors suspended in the water. This process uses activated charcoal to cleanse the caffeine from the water. All decaffeinated coffee has some caffeine remaining; the amount can range from negligible to thirty-five milligrams per cup. Whether decaffeinated or not, after all of the processing has occurred and specialty coffee roasters have made their selections, the beans are then bagged, most often in 132-pound jute or sisal bags. However, before bagging, our roasters, Ecco/Intelligentsia, take one extra step to maintain the integrity of the green coffee. Sorted and hulled beans are carefully packaged at origin in plastic grain-pro inner liner bags that protect the green beans from moisture transfer. This extra measure guarantees that the delicate flavors, nuances, and vibrancy of the green beans remain. The jute or sisal bag then adds an extra layer of protection to our select beans.

There is, as always seems the case with coffee, one exception to this packaging process. Some reserve lots from Kenya and the Cup of Excellence program are vacuum-packed in Mylar bags at origin and transferred to cardboard boxes for shipping. It is felt that vacuum-packing offers first-rate protection, ensuring the exceptional flavor and shelf life of green coffee beans.

Whether bags or boxes, appropriate packaging is extremely important, as the beans must be protected from heat, light, oxygen, moisture, and contaminants in the air during shipping. With the most common packing and shipping method, the green bean–filled bags are placed in metal shipping containers and begin their journey to the cup. After the long processing period, the time it takes for the beans to travel to the roaster and onto the specialty coffee bar is relatively short—usually no more than a month. And, as much care will be committed to the roasting as has gone into the growing and processing.

COFFEE FACTS:

Coffee is traded as a commodity (symbol KT) on the New York Mercantile Exchange (NYMEX), bought and sold by investors and speculators with contract deliveries in March, May, July, September, and December.

ROASTING to PERFECTION

ECCO CAFFÈ

As we have seen, long before the beans are delivered to the barista, very small samples of lightly roasted beans are "cupped" (see pages 30 and 38) to determine the qualities and/or faults of an entire batch. In the specialty coffee trade, this is done in a cooperative tasting between the buyer and either the farmer or skilled cuppers at the final point of processing. Once cupped and selected, the beans are shipped to the roasting facility—in the case of all **joe** coffees, that would be either at Ecco Caffè in Santa Rosa, California, or at its sister company in Chicago, Intelligentsia Roasting Works. The beans continue to be cupped throughout the profiling process to determine the roasting approach that maximizes the quality inherent in the bean. Although an optimal roast profile can be met on the inaugural roast, it often takes many cuppings to determine the perfect roast for each coffee.

Cupping coffee is an art, one almost unknown to otherwise skilled culinary professionals. This tasting method is used by specialty coffee growers and by all buyers, roasters, and baristas to evaluate the flavor profile and aroma of individual coffees from a specific region. It is an essential element of the roasting process because, by continually cupping, the cupper learns to distinguish all of the desirable characteristics of a specific specialty coffee and how the roast can emphasize them.

The purpose of roasting coffee is to bring out the inherent flavors of the green bean. Although the green beans contain many of the same qualities and chemicals as roasted beans, they do not have the flavors. The characteristic notes that identify a specific coffee can only be gained through the chemical reactions brought about by proper roasting. The roasting process should be done as close to when the brewed coffee will be consumed, since roasted coffee beans quickly begin to lose their fresh taste and the flavor profile begins to rapidly diminish. Interestingly,

Roasted beans

green beans are very dense and flavorless and would be almost impossible to process into ground coffee.

Cooperative ventures between producers and buyers have increased the specificity of each producer/region/micro-lot, varietal, and terroir (including soil type, elevation, climate, etc.), while processing, sorting, milling, and shipping improvements have allowed the specialty coffee industry to identify high-quality

COFFEE FACTS:

Currently, Brazil is the largest coffee producer in the world. In 2006, of the forty-four million bags of coffee produced there, twenty-seven million were exported. However, in 1928, Brazil's entire economy collapsed due to overproduction.

coffees. Through new and innovative advances made by buyers and producers, quality continues to improve, and producers are rewarded with higher prices and recognition as true artisans in their field. All of these details lead to nuances in the cup. On the consumer side, these changes require an educated palate that can appreciate these nuances. An analogy that is often made is to the improvements in quality wine production and educated consumers.

Green beans

Once the beans arrive at the roastery, the roasting process begins by using a small test roaster to set the temperature, time, and air flow. Sample roasting is valuable in determining the quality of the samples submitted by farmers and importers. However, quality roasters know that sample roasting can be helpful in understanding what a production roast *might* taste like. Because the sample roasting equipment is so much smaller than the production roasting equipment, the sample roasting can produce variable results. Sample roasts are evaluated to determine the potential flavor of a production roast; however, the qualities that emerge in the sample roast do not always translate into those of the larger production roasts. This is where the skill of the roaster comes to play.

This test batch is cupped and scored, numerically, for sweetness, acidity, flavor, body, and finish with each category numbered from five to ten. Once all of the categories have been scored and totaled, the number forty is added, after which the cupper can add "Cuppers' Points" so that they can adjust their score based on overall impression being greater than the sum of its parts, altogether resulting in the

Imperfect beans

final score. The highest total score is one hundred, and it has rarely been reached. In order to be considered a "specialty" coffee, a coffee must score a minimum of eighty points with eighty-three being the benchmark. To qualify for the Cup of Excellence auction, the coffee must score eighty-four points. Cup of Excellence Presidential Award coffees are further distinguished with a score of ninety points and above. When we cup at **joe** (see pages 30 and 38), we do not score coffees since this rating has already been done at the time of purchase. We simply judge through descriptive phrases, which help the barista explain the nuances of a coffee to the customer.

Since it is the role of the roasting process to ensure that a coffee's distinguishing features are highlighted, the process is part science and part art. Observing small-batch specialty coffee being roasted is an extraordinary experience. Although the process is mechanical, the roaster stands continual guard, listening for the popping noises that indicate the various points of doneness and monitoring the time, temperature, gas level, air flow, aroma, and appearance of the roasting beans. Throughout the day, the roasted beans are cupped to

ensure that the roaster has maintained the desired profile. The ongoing roast profiling is essential as coffees can change as they rest further in the roaster or undergo environmental changes. As you can imagine, to do justice to the hard work of the producer, profiling is exceedingly important, particularly with the expensive micro-lots that may consist of only a few bags of green beans.

Once the roasted beans are tumbled onto the cooling bin, the art of the skilled roaster is evident. As a turning mechanism slowly aerates the cooling beans, the roaster carefully eyes the batch and, by hand, picks out any beans that don't measure up to the defined standard. They might be cracked, suffer from mill damage, be too small, or be "quakers," which appear as beans that are much more lightly roasted but are, in fact, cherries that were underdeveloped at harvest. These are all imperfections that only a trained eye can see, and the process can only be done at a small-batch facility by a highly skilled roaster.

At the small Ecco Caffè roastery in Santa Rosa, our **joe** coffee beans are done in extremely small batches. These roasts are done in a 1999 Dietrich drum roaster that holds only sixteen pounds of green beans. The roaster must run

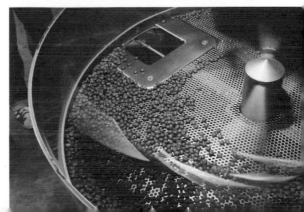

The ART OF CUP- PING

BREAKDOWN OF A PROFESSIONAL ROASTER/CUPPER'S COFFEE SCORING

95–100	Clean, sweet, all characteristics exceptional, unbeatable
90–94	Clean, sweet, all characteristics terrific with multiple exceptional qualities
85–89	Clean, sweet, enjoyable characteristics with one or two excellent definable qualities
80–84	Necessary rating to designate specialty coffee; clean with mostly pleasant qualities
75–79	Cannot be designated as specialty coffee; negative qualities distract from the desired flavor
70–74	Elements that are aggressively unpleasant
65–69	Significant, outstanding defect
Less than 65	Totally undesirable; undrinkable

continually throughout the day and, often, into the evening to produce the ever-changing and growing amount of coffee we use at **joe** weekly. Larger batches are roasted at Intelligentsia Roasting Works in Chicago in vintage Gothat machines. Along with Amanda Byron, we frequently visit the roasteries and are partners in the ongoing tasting of the product before it is released to our stores.

Many types of roasting machines exist, but all **joe** coffees are roasted in drum roasters. The process begins with the green beans placed in a hopper that lowers them into a drum. The heat source is under the drum, and as the drum turns, the beans are tumbled and evenly roasted. The roaster can watch the process through a small window called a sightglass and, from time to time, remove a few beans using a trier to gauge the degree of doneness.

Green beans are generally roasted between 380°F and 400°F. The entire process takes 11 to 14½ minutes with the first crack (the popping noise associated with roasting beans) occurring at 8 to 11 minutes. During the intense heat of the short roasting process, the sugars in the beans become caramelized, giving the coffee its ultimate flavor. Although the beans swell during roasting, they also lose volume so that the starting weight drops by 15 to 18 percent.

There are, of course, varying degrees of roast. It is up to the roaster and the barista to determine the roast profile that best highlights each particular coffee. At **joe** we work closely with our roastery to determine the coffees that best meet our profile. The same attention to quality is given to the roasting of all of our beans, caffeinated or not, so much so, that we feel that **joe** decaf sings with the same deliciousness as all of our regular coffees. A lightly roasted coffee will range in color from cinnamon to milk chocolate while a dark roast can be almost ebony with a shiny exterior. Lightly roasted coffees are generally more acidic and bright tasting, reflecting their origin, while very dark roasts can be almost bitter on the palate. It should go without saying that we prefer the lighter roasts!

When the beans are extremely dark, the coffee will often taste more of the

COFFEE FACTS:

The United States imports every single coffee bean except for a small amount grown in Hawaii, the only state with the weather and soil conducive to coffee production.

roasting than of the complexities of the bean. Although you will not find dark roasts at **joe,** it is interesting to note that the darker the roast the less the caffeine content. The lessening of caffeine occurs during the longer roasting period where the inherent oils are drawn to the surface of the bean.

In the current rage to return to the earth, some roasters in the United States have gone back to roasting green beans over fruit wood, a traditional method that is

still practiced in some areas of Italy. These traditionalists feel that the smoke from the fruity wood adds an intriguing dimension to the roasted beans, imparting an otherwise unfound sweetness as well as enhancing the bean's natural essence.

Immediately after roasting, the beans are packed according to their origin, with the exception of our **joe** house coffee and our espresso blends, which are normally a blending of various beans to achieve the notes that we feel best identify a **joe** flavor profile. Each bean in each blend is labeled by origin with as much care as the single origin filter offerings. This is again where art intersects science as the roaster, working with the barista, carefully unites the qualities of the beans that will together create a distinctive cup of **joe.**

Freshly roasted specialty coffee beans have a brief shelf life, optimally no more than two weeks. Once roasted, coffee beans begin to stale quite rapidly. They must be kept from exposure to light, heat, moisture, and oxygen to ensure that they stay fresh for even this minimal length of time. At **joe** our beans are packed in one-way valve bags with a pressure-relieving button that allows naturally accumulating carbon dioxide to escape. The insulation keeps the beans as fresh as possible during the optimal storage period. However, once opened, the entire bag should be placed in an airtight container. We do grind beans to order but suggest that consumers grind only the amount they need immediately, since ground coffee quickly becomes stale. Under no circumstances should the beans be refrigerated since they will pick up the undesirable odors of the refrigerator or freezer, damaging their purity.

IT'S ALL IN THE TASTE

The ESSENCE of the CUP:
IT'S ALL in the TASTE

Once the bags of roasted coffee are shipped to **joe,** our baristas undergo an intense learning experience as they familiarize their palate with the flavors of the individual coffees. Since we rely on freshness and seasonality, our origin coffees have a quick turnover. The Brazilian you loved on Monday may be replaced with a very different Kenyan by Friday. Throughout the ongoing transition of getting what coffees are in season, Amanda Byron leads the cupping sessions and educational seminars for the **joe** staff as well as directs our classes, which are open to the public at our in-house coffee university.

When cupping and tasting, we look for complexity, richness, and perfect balance in the brew. Complexity occurs when the taster identifies diverse flavors commingling, richness might be identified as the roundness of the body, and balance is the comprehension of all of the desired elements required for a specific blend. These characteristics come together in a brew that is 98 percent water and 1 to 2 percent flavor and color.

When combined with hot water, about 28 percent of coffee is soluble; however, we do not want to leech out all 28 percent as this would make the brewed coffee acrid and bitter. Precise brewing will only extract about 22 percent of the coffee solids, leaving the bright, sweet, caramel-like cup that we desire. The actual percentage determines what is usually known as the "strength" of a cup of coffee.

Cupping takes practice. The first few attempts can be awkward, but once you get into the swing of it, cupping can be a lot of fun as well as educational. Much like wine tasting, it is an old process that has strict rules and regulations that are followed throughout the world. The coffee to be cupped is ground and carefully weighed. At **joe** cuppings we use 12 grams of coffee, ground fairly coarse in a 7-ounce bowl or cup.

The first job is to experience the dry aroma of the coffee. Next step, add hot water, just off the boil, to the top of the cup, letting it brew for four minutes. Take a moment to experience the aroma of the wet grounds, then "break the crust." This is done by pushing a spoon into the grounds (which have formed a crust) carefully to the back of the

The Specialty Coffee Association Of America
FLAVOR COLOR WHEEL

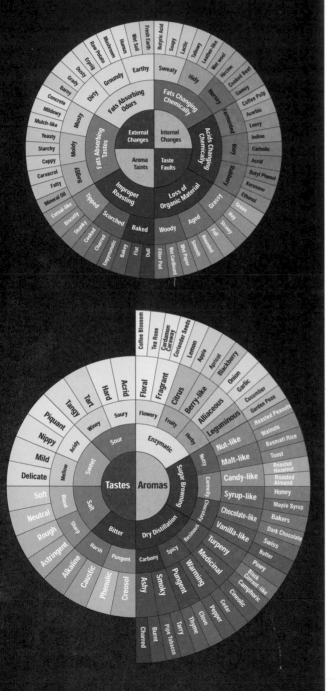

cup. The cupper will place her nose right above the crust to get the full measure of the aromatic characteristics trapped just under the surface of the coffee.

After the crust has been broken, the grounds then steep for anywhere from another 5 to 10 minutes depending on how much the cupper wants the coffee to cool. After skimming the foam and minimal grinds from the top of the cup, tasting begins as small amounts of coffee are taken in with loud, noisy, inelegant slurps. This sounds easy enough, but it takes time and practice to slurp properly, allowing the coffee to be sprayed across the entire palate. Once tasted, the coffee is usually spit into another cup so as to avoid overcaffeination. Interestingly enough the flavors change and intensify as the coffee cools. It is often easier to discern all of the qualities sought when the coffee is lukewarm. In fact, it is standard practice to first taste the coffee when it is hot, but not scalding, and then go back for another taste when the coffee cools.

40

CUPPING

POURING

COFFEE FACTS:

Coffee is one of the most complex substances that we consume, clocking in with nearly one thousand aromatic compounds with more being constantly discovered.

Although each cupper will find her reaction to a specific coffee to be very personal, with the aromas occasionally bringing up long forgotten memories, there are some generalizations that can cover the primary sensual experiences of coffee cupping. On the following pages we will attempt to give a brief overview of the various fragrances and aromas, tastes, and mouth-feel that predominate when cupping specialty coffees. These will give you the base for cupping your own freshly brewed coffee.

FRAGRANCE/AROMA

The fragrance is defined as the aroma you inhale after the beans have been ground and placed in the cup. This is your first sense of the flavors you might experience in the finished cup. The aroma follows as it comes from the smells that arise once the ground coffee has been covered with hot water. Breathing in these complex aromas furthers your sensory expectations. Although not limited to these varying bouquets, the following are among the many aromatic sensations you might experience. Some of them are very pleasant while others might be off-putting. Some of these associations are only experienced by a professional taster, and we, as a group, have not come close to familiarity with all of them. When a seasoned buyer or roaster cups, his refined palate can judge when, if, and how the off-putting aromas will impact the finished cup.

FOOD ASSOCIATIONS

Herb/Grass: Sensations include all fresh-cut herbs, especially parsley, tarragon, and basil, freshly mown grass or hay, bursting spring green foliage, dewy grass, the air of a bright spring day.

COFFEE FACTS:

There are about 130 million coffee drinkers in the United States.

WAKE UP
WITH A
BARISTA

Fruit: Berries and citrus fruits are the most common aromas sensed. The sweet, juicy aroma of mashed ripe berries (usually a specific type) is a frequent denominator, while both the smell and taste of citrus, particularly the sweeter fruits, often follow from the fragrance through to the final taste.

Chocolate: All manner of chocolate—from cocoa powder to unsweetened baking chocolate—is frequently found in the fragrance and aroma of specialty coffees. When milk chocolate is smelled, the coffee is often described as simply sweet-smelling.

Spice: Generally only those spices that are termed sweet, such as cinnamon, cloves, allspice, and cardamom, are found. Although the scent of savory spices can be noticed, it is usually described specifically, such as black pepper or ginger.

Caramel: Caramel-like is often the first descriptor a cupper will experience, but it is the aroma of perfectly caramelized sugar that the cupper is seeking. The aroma of burnt sugar, though, would be an unpleasant note throughout the coffee.

Cereal: Both the aroma of raw or uncooked grains as well as cooked or roasted ones, such as oats, wheat, or corn, can be noticed. For professional cupping, this particular fragrance/aroma has been grouped with malt and toasted bread aromas into one category, a grain-type aroma.

Toast: The aromas sensed include freshly baked sweet breads, toast, and warm out-of-the-oven yeast-based breads and rolls.

Malt: The fragrance and aroma range from warm biscuit-like to deep earthy grain flavor; sometimes even the defining malt characteristics of beer are sensed.

Nut: The all-encompassing aroma of fresh and/or roasted nuts often defines specialty coffee. However, any note of rancidity or bitterness indicates a poor quality coffee.

Wine: Everything about the sensations of drinking a fine wine—aroma, flavor, body—comes together when this fragrance/aroma is experienced. This generally indicates fruity qualities and a refined acidic note in the finished cup. However, at the opposite end, the fragrance/aroma should not be one of sour fermentation.

COFFEE FACTS:

Around the world, about twelve billion pounds of coffee and four hundred billion cups of coffee are consumed annually.

Burnt food: The dark, earthy, rather unpleasant aroma when foods are overcooked may be experienced.

Rancid fat: The aroma may seem like the oxidation of nut and animal fats. This aroma is not necessarily a sign of deterioration in the coffee, but of a general strong note.

Rotten food: The aromas emanating from decaying vegetables or vegetation or other non-fat products again can indicate strength rather than deterioration in coffee.

NOTES OF NATURE

Floral: The cupper may sense the bare scent of almost any flower, but often sweet flowers such as jasmine or honeysuckle, occasionally rose. Of all the fragrances and aromas, this one is rarely experienced in the finished cup.

Woody: Aromas include damp forest floor, dry wood, wooden barrels, even old cardboard, particularly if wet.

Dirt: Freshly dug earth, humus, damp soil, a soaking, watered garden may all be experienced, but a moldy, earth-like aroma is undesirable.

Tobacco: The aroma should be of fresh tobacco, only.

Burnt wood: The fragrance/aroma of smoke from burning wood often indicates a bean that has been overroasted.

Animal: The general smells of an animal—wet fur, a just-raced horse, leather, dried hides—may be sensed. Again, this is used to describe intense coffee notes and is not considered undesirable.

OTHER ASSOCIATIONS

Medicinal: The fragrance/aroma may be of a just-opened pill bottle, a hospital corridor, a doctor's office—all familiar, but not necessarily pleasant associations.

Rubber: A cupper may sense the smell of burning rubber, hot tires, and rubber bands. Interestingly, this aroma is required in some coffees and, as such, is not considered undesirable but can be a characteristic of darker roasted coffee.

Ash: This is a scent one normally shies away from—a dirty ashtray, a smoker's fingers, or the accumulation of ashes in a fireplace. Again, this is not an undesirable aroma but one used to indicate the degree of roast.

TASTES

Acidity comes from the hint of brightness you experience with a sweet, clean coffee. It is acidity that offers the most captivating floral or fruit flavors. The perception of high acidity in some coffees is correlated with the characteristics of citrus fruits. In a specialty coffee, the perceived acidity can range all over the map—from intense to almost nonexistent, from soft and round to irritable, from sophisticated to untamed; you name it, acidity has been so described. Acidic notes are best experienced once a coffee has cooled to lukewarm.

Acid: This is not the unpleasant taste often associated with sour acids, but a quite refined sharp, agreeable flavor that frequently exemplifies coffees from specific regions.

COFFEE FACTS:

The first wholesale coffee roasting company in America was founded in 1790 at what is believed to be 4 Great Dock Street (now Pearl Street) in New York City. That same year also saw the first newspaper advertisement for coffee.

Bitter: This is one flavor that the roasting and brewing techniques impact. It is one of the primary taste notes in coffee that is identified by a mixture of quinine, caffeine, and particular alkaloids.

Saline: This is another premier taste that is identified by sodium chloride and other salts.

Sour: When tasting, these notes are often confused with the more pleasing acidic notes. Sour notes will be much more bitter and sharp, rather like vinegar, and can be the result of fermented coffee.

Sweet: This is one of the best and most desirable tastes, used to define any coffee that has absolutely no off-flavor. It is the one characteristic that often separates great coffee from good. It is often found in partnership with acidity and, in turn, creates the perfect balance necessary to mellow out the intense acid. It brings forth the sweet notes of caramel, fruit, and/or chocolate.

BODY OR MOUTH-FEEL

This is simply how the coffee feels when sipped and rolled on the tongue. It is often the most difficult trait for beginning cuppers to grasp. It is best to think of it as the weight of the coffee and the texture you feel in your mouth. A good example would be the varying weights of heavy cream, whole milk, and skim milk on the palate. Great specialty coffee should leave a lasting fullness on the palate, never a thin, watery feel.

FLAVOR

This is the complete sensation of all of the elements of a particular coffee coming together in the mouth.

FINISH

Great specialty coffee has a pleasant, lingering aftertaste. This is the lasting impression and is often far more memorable than the first sip. The perfect finish is one that is sweet, free of imploding elements, and lasts for at least ten seconds after the coffee has been swallowed. Most of all, the finish should produce the defined flavor of the coffee. If the coffee leaves an unpleasant, astringent aftertaste and a dry mouth, it is not good coffee and should be discarded. And, if the coffee is neutral in flavor and leaves no aftertaste, it would be deemed unacceptable.

COFFEE CUPPING CHART

The chart opposite is a basic cupping chart and can be used by the individual taster to enter his or her analysis of each of the defined coffee characteristics through the specified segment of the cupping process. This process will be fully described and illustrated so that the reader can "cup" at home to determine the quality of purchased beans.

Over the past few decades, almost twenty thousand studies have investigated the benefits and/or drawbacks of coffee consumption. Whether such news impacts the buying and brewing habits of **joe** consumers, we can't say, but it has been found that coffee does contain a number of excellent health perks while coming with a few health warnings. Because of the antioxidant compounds in coffee, moderate coffee consumption can aid in the reduction of risk of Alzheimer's disease, dementia, and stroke, while frequent coffee drinking can lower the risk of diabetes, prostate cancer, and liver disease. In fact, it seems that the more coffee you drink the less your chance of contracting liver cancer, although just the opposite occurs with heart disease as it is believed that too much caffeine combats the effects of the antioxidants. The warnings center on the consumption of too much caffeine, resulting in a "caffeine buzz" that can disturb sleep and concentration as well as cause anxiety and irritability. Although doctors and studies note that pregnant women can consume up to 300 milligrams of caffeine a day, roughly one large cup or three espressos, at **joe** we find that a lot of our customers who are pregnant or nursing switch to decaf for the duration.

	FRAGRANCE	AROMA/BREAK	ACIDITY	FLAVOR	BODY	AFTERTASTE
COFFEE #1:						
COFFEE #2:						
COFFEE #3:						

FRAGRANCE: The smell of beans after grinding

AROMA/BREAK: The smell of the coffee after water is added

TASTE: The flavor of the coffee

BODY: The feel of the coffee in your mouth

AFTERTASTE: The vapors and flavors that remain after swallowing

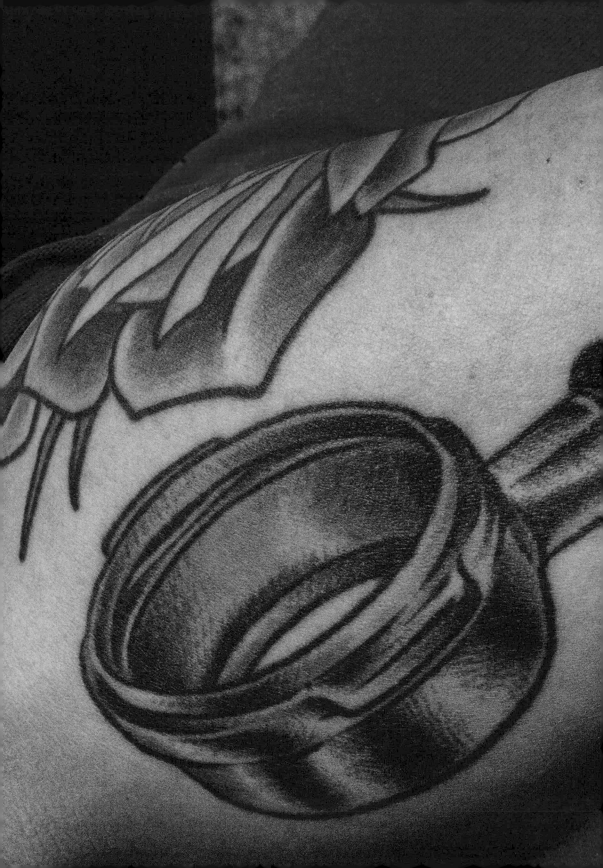

The COMMUNITY of COFFEE

The most amazing thing about being in the specialty coffee business is the noncompetitiveness of it. Of course, each farmer, each buyer, each roaster, each company, each barista, each drinker has his or her own unique objective, but by and large, we are all working together to improve the quality of coffee from seed to cup. At **joe**, the goal is really quite simple. We encourage all of our employees to experience the coffee world at its fullest, and that means we are serious about hospitality not only in our coffee bars but throughout the industry. The fact is that social networking happens throughout the coffee world.

The international specialty coffee community is a tight-knit group of committed growers, buyers, roasters, entrepreneurs, baristas, and drinkers who are determined to source, purchase, roast, serve, and drink the world's finest coffees. The specialty coffee trade is a dynamic and exciting global industry that is expanding rapidly and is dedicated to combining cup quality with sustainability and social and economic responsibility. Those involved always end up in the same seat—enjoying a cup of excellence with friends, coworkers, or even the "competition."

For us, the present leader in the social network of coffee is Ecco/Intelligentsia, the current roasters of **joe** beans. Intelligentsia began as a coffee bar in Chicago and then leaped to Los Angeles, growing to seven coffee bars and purchasing the esteemed roaster Ecco Caffè. The coffee community views this combined group with near reverence. Although we support the philosophy of our premier roasters (which absolutely mirrors our own), we also acknowledge the creativity and convictions of other coffee bars and/or roasters. Among our friendly competitors are Stumptown, roasters and bars with origins in Portland, Oregon, and now with an international presence; Espresso Vivace, a Seattle bar and roaster that is often credited with starting the third-wave coffee movement; Octane Coffee in Atlanta; and Ritual Coffee Roasters, a leading San Francisco roaster with signature bars, along with many others on the growing national and international scene.

Here we introduce you to some participants in the international link of growers, buyers, roasters, coffee bar owners, baristas, and, of course, consumers, the most dedicated coffee connoisseurs. Each one shares his or her own view of the world of coffee as it stands today.

BARTH ANDERSON

PARTNER, BARRINGTON COFFEE ROASTING COMPANY

The birth of **joe**: *"With great fondness I recall the early days of unctuous, up-dosed American espresso in the West Village. It's the spring of 2003, and Jonathan and I are walking around inside of a recently vacant Laundromat, hardly more than a hole in the wall. We are planning the interior layout of a café that would soon boast the cutting edge engineering of a Synesso Cyncra in the locale that would come to be known as joe Waverly. It was a pioneering time with all of the risks and the spoils that come along with it. Threats from industry dinosaurs, struggles to establish nontraditional commercial infrastructure, graciously offset by the reception of a new kind of customer, lots of new customers, and the glory of a popular press ready to celebrate it all. Barrington Gold flowed vigorously through the veins of New York. New York embraced us. It was quite a time."*

60

MICHAEL PHILLIPS

**2009 UNITED STATES BARISTA CHAMPION/
2010 WORLD BARISTA CHAMPION/
COFOUNDER, HANDSOME COFFEE ROASTERS**

"People often ask me what the best coffeemaker out there is, and the answer is rather simple. The best coffeemaker out there is just a person who cares about the cup. Someone who is willing to invest the time and effort needed to make a proper brew will always be better than any machine or gimmick on the market."

DREW CATTLIN

**PRIMARY ROASTER, STUMPTOWN
COFFEE ROASTERS**

"The way we prepare coffee is changing rapidly. In the past, we had no idea just how sweet it could be. As my knowledge grows, I am finding that coffee is the most complex food on the planet."

AMANDA BYRON

VICE PRESIDENT AND DIRECTOR OF COFFEE, joe

"I certainly don't want to get too political or preachy about it, but I hope that with the next cup of coffee you consume, you put just a bit more thought into where it came from and think about all of the people who had a hand in getting it into your cup."

STEPHEN MORRISSEY

2008 IRISH AND WORLD BARISTA CHAMPION

"I won't pretend to hate caffeine, but I wish people cared more about flavor and less about function."

STEVE MIERISCH

NICARAGUAN COFFEE FARM FAMILY,
ECCO CAFFÈ/INTELLIGENTSIA COFFEE,
CHICAGO

"Because I come from a coffee farming family, it is my goal to bridge the gap between the farmer and the consumer through education. At Ecco/Intelligentsia, we strive to provide as much information as possible about every bag we sell."

DAVID LATOURELLE

CUSTOMER SUPPORT, INTELLIGENTSIA COFFEE

"Though some might say hyperbole is my middle name, I'm not usually prone to excessive praise. Working with joe, training their baristas, tasting their coffees, and seeing the care they give to both coffee and people: awesome!"

MIKKI KOSKIE

BARISTA/MANAGER, joe WAVERLY MANAGER

"I think that one of the reasons that coffee bars have become so popular is the sociability associated with having a cup of coffee. It is almost ritualistic—you gather, you sip, you relax, and you connect."

GINA DEPALMA

PASTRY CHEF, BABBO RESTAURANT, NEW YORK CITY

"The aroma of espresso bubbling up from the battered Bialetti pot on my stove instantly transports me from New York to Italy. I close my eyes and imagine the back streets of my old neighborhood in Rome, where the air is perfumed with brewing espresso every morning; the rich fragrance of roasted Arabica spills out of kitchen windows and bar doorways. Anywhere but Rome, I take it with hot milk, a bit of sugar, and a huge dash of melancholy."

RANDY GARUTTI

COFFEE LOVER, UNION SQUARE HOSPITALITY GROUP, CHIEF OPERATING OFFICER, SHAKE SHACK

"joe is my community center. The place I go with my kids, with my wife, with my coworkers—whenever we need a real cup of coffee. It's the place I feel most at home, away from home. joe is New York at its best—people from all walks of life, coming together, enjoying each other's company."

WILLIAM GROSS

ROASTER, STUMPTOWN, BROOKLYN

"Coffee is constantly changing, and that keeps it incredibly fascinating to me."

COFFEE FACTS:

In 1453, Turkish law made it legal for a woman to divorce her husband if he failed to provide her with her daily quota of coffee.

ANDREW BARNETT

FOUNDER ECCO CAFFÈ, SANTA ROSA, CALIFORNIA

"We are in the golden age of coffee. Never before have we had access to better quality coffees direct from the farm or greater understanding on how to prepare them. We're in the early stages—it's only going to get better and better."

LIZ CLAYTON

NEW YORK-BASED COFFEE WRITER

"Before I moved to New York, I was drawn in by its quickly exploding coffee scene, one of the anchors of which was joe. I'd regularly battle through squadrons of cramped tables at Waverly to eat cupcakes baked by Amy Sedaris and take touristy photos of my macchiato. Watching joe grow up alongside NYC's coffee scene has been inspiring—it's no small thing to be an institution that's willing to evolve with the times. The coffee keeps getting better—and Waverly is just as crowded!"

AMBER FOX

FORMERLY COFFEE CONTROL/GREEN COFFEE
MANAGER, ECCO CAFFÈ, SANTA ROSA, CALIFORNIA

"As a coffee professional, one of the most magical moments is when a person tastes a truly delicious coffee for the very first time. Their eyes light up, a slow smile spreads across their face, and you know that you've just helped surpass all their expectations for what a cup of coffee can be. The chance to facilitate that moment, to shift the paradigm of coffee as a daily caffeination mechanism and reveal it as a transcendent culinary experience, is what we aim to bring to as many people as possible. Each moment like that first sip helps to fuel our work to further improve quality at each step of the process—growing, picking, processing, sorting, shipping, roasting, and preparation. Specialty coffee has the unique power to bring producers, roasters, and consumers together through their love and passion for a small flavorful seed with huge potential. Ecco is honored to work with a company like joe that epitomizes this passion and the ambassadorial spirit that propels specialty coffee to ever greater heights."

VIVIAN TONG

SPECIALTY COFFEE FAN/
SMALL BUSINESS OWNER

"Once you taste joe coffee, you can't drink anything else— even when the line is long!"

67

EZRA SEPTIMUS

NINE-YEAR-OLD COFFEE-SAVVY NEW YORKER (WITH DAD, MATTHEW)

"Daddy is very grouchy if he doesn't have his cup of coffee in the morning."

AMY HATTEMER

BARISTA/MANAGER, joe GRAND CENTRAL STATION

"At joe, some days it feels like we are trying to right injustice in the world with each cup served, exposing our customers to beautiful coffees cultivated by extraordinarily hardworking men and women from around the world; other days it just feels nice to know we work for a company that lets us be ourselves and drink coffee with our buddies."

LOUIS POORE

URNEX BRANDS

"As a group, we're driven by quality: quality at the farm, quulily in the cup, quality in the bars, quality in our interactions with customers. Quality has come to stand as the basis for our relation to coffee, itself."

PETER HOFFMAN

CHEF/OWNER, SAVOY RESTAURANT, NEW YORK CITY

"joe coffee hits the spot after an early Saturday morning Greenmarket run. I particularly appreciate the 'luste of place' in joe's single origin coffees. A good cup of 'joe' requires careful sourcing and care for the beans all along the supply chain."

RICHARD NIETO

OWNER, SWEETLEAF CAFÉ, LONG ISLAND CITY,
NEW YORK

"As baristas we are given the privilege of preparing and serving the final product to our customers. We should look to honor all the people from the coffee picker to the roaster who have worked so hard to make great coffee possible."

ERIN MEISTER

COFFEE PROFESSIONAL/WRITER, COUNTER CULTURE COFFEE, NEW YORK CITY

"Coffee might not feed the body, but it definitely feeds the soul: There's nothing like that first steaming mug first thing in the morning, the shared afternoon cup between friends, the joke that passes between a customer and his favorite barista, or the shy question, 'Do you want to get a coffee sometime?' What else do we eat or drink that can carry us through such a day and create so many different, beautiful little connections between people? Coffee is food: soul food."

FARAH KHAWAJA

BARISTA, joe GRAND CENTRAL STATION

"Being from New York, I can't imagine working in any other store. joe Grand Central Station epitomizes the energy of New York City. It's intense, it's fun, it's crazy. Coffee moves so fast, but like the true New York attitude, we refuse to sacrifice the integrity of the cup for anyone or anything."

DANIELLA BONANNO

LEGAL SERVICES DIRECTOR, FC USA INC./COFFEE FANATIC

"Life is too short to drink bad coffee. joe jump-starts my days!"

NICOLE SLAVEN KAUFMANN

FORMER OWNER, DORA, LOWER EAST SIDE COFFEE BAR, NEW YORK CITY

"I've always been a morning person, even when I've been a night owl. Nothing makes me shine more than seeing customers' faces each day, taking care of them, from listening to their coffee order to seeing them receiving it. Coffee doesn't make the world go 'round, but it sure puts a spin on its axis."

LEE HARRISON

TRAINER, MANAGER AND BARISTA,
joe COLUMBIA UNIVERSITY

"Not only are baristas proficient in the craft of coffee as part of the endeavor to liberate the senses, we are expert liaisons between consumers and producers, the contact point for a global operation. Baristas are stewards of the 'third place,' nurturers of culture, and mediators of the coffee shop as a social nexus. Coffee is a gateway drug."

72

NICOLAS KARLSON

PRODUCER, joe UPPER WEST SIDE REGULAR

"So here's the story. . . . Just out of college I was dating this girl, and it came to the moment that all relationships come to. The conversation of love. The question was, is there anything that I love? I responded, 'Of course, I love espresso.' A look of shock and anger crossed her face. I continued. 'I can live without almost everything. I have very few needs in this world. But there is not a day that goes by that I can or am willing to go without espresso. That seems like love to me.' That said, the relationship did not go too far past that moment. But, my relationship with espresso is still strong."

COFFEE FACTS:

In 1675, a year after receiving the Women's Petition Against Coffee, the king of England closed all coffeehouses for ten days in response to the petition, which accused coffeehouses of excluding women, causing neglect by husbands and sapping the men of their sex drive.

ANNA UTEVSKY

BARISTA, MANAGER, **joe** UPPER WEST
SIDE/CHEF/WRITER

*"My favorite coffees remind me
of great fiction, amazing in their
singularity; clear expressions of
place, people, and time."*

CHARROW

BARISTA/ARTIST, **joe**

*"I never thought a job would help define me as a person. How can you not love
a place where tattooed freaks and suits can carry on mundane conversations?"*

ADAM ROBERTS

AUTHOR, CREATOR, THE AMATEUR GOURMET
(WWW.AMATEURGOURMET.COM)

"I first went to joe on a quest for a nice, sunny place to do work. Little did I know that the coffee there would spoil me for all other coffee: I'd never had espresso so flavorful and potent, or milk-based coffee drinks with designs so lovingly shaped. Now, rarely does a day pass without a visit to joe. It's one of my favorite places in New York."

GREG AND ELLEN WEYANDT

FREQUENT joe VISITORS FROM MINNESOTA

"First it was coffee at joe. Then it became our New York community."

MIKE WHITE

COFFEE CONSULTANT/AUTHOR/BLOGGER OF SHOTZOMBIES.COM

"New York is one of the biggest melting pots in the world, and nowhere is that more apparent than the neighborhood coffee bar where people from every socioeconomic background gather and interact."

SCOUT ROSE

BARISTA, *joe*

"My favorite thing about being in coffee is the endless opportunity for learning. I feel like I could study coffee every day for the rest of my life and still have more to discover."

WILL ZUCKERMAN

NEWBORN

"I have been a joe customer since before I was born. My mom loves her latte—decaf now, but back to caffeine when I'm up and running."

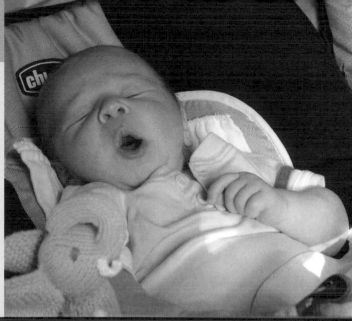

HUMBERTO RICARDO

OWNER, THIRD RAIL COFFEE,
NEW YORK CITY

"My favorite thing about espresso is its lingering aftertaste when properly extracted. A tiny beverage consumed in seconds will yield amazing flavors for up to a half an hour or more, ironically making it the ultimate 'to-go' coffee."

SAM LIPP

GENERAL MANAGER, UNION SQUARE CAFÉ, NEW YORK CITY

"With such increased and fierce competition for your ritualistic, caffeinated pleasure throughout the city, Jonathan Rubinstein and joe continue to champion more than just what is in the cup. Not only is the coffee delicious, but it is reliably prepared by expertly trained staff, who possess intimate knowledge of their product while consistently embodying the warmth and humble graciousness that has become a hallmark for the banner under which they pull their shots. I LOVE joe!!!!"

VALERIE VON FERSTEL

A PARISIAN IN NEW YORK

"Voltaire wrote le bonheur est une mot complexe compose de petits plaisirs, *which translates to 'happiness is a complex word composed of small pleasures' . . . and for me coffee is one of these pleasures."*

MAKING "JOE"
TASTE LIKE JOE

The BREW: MAKING "JOE" TASTE LIKE JOE

SEASONAL HOUSE

PAPUA NEW GUINEA AGODA ESTATE

Because we are committed to using only the freshest, most full-bodied beans at **joe,** all of the coffees we offer change frequently based on seasonality and the work we do with our roaster. For instance, the components of our house coffee blend change based on which beans are available and fresh. However, the profile of the blend's flavor is always reliable. Whatever their origin, the beans are all freshly roasted so that only the highest flavor profile is offered in the cup.

In addition to the beans we begin with, it is essential that every cup is made with the perfect brew in mind. Amanda Byron leads our educational forums for all **joe** employees so that new blends, techniques, and machinery become part of their coffee DNA. Every barista who joins us goes through a long training period, often beginning with a stint as a barback (technically *barback* is the term for a bartender's assistant, but we use it to describe new employees whose first job is behind the coffee bar performing general cleanup and assisting the baristas however needed) and with many sessions at our espresso machine. But, no matter how much training we give or how revolutionary new techniques and machinery might be, our mantra is "everything comes back to taste." To make certain that taste is the preeminent goal, both the brewed coffees and espresso are tasted by our baristas throughout the day, every day.

The professional environment created by the barista team helps us examine the various types of coffees and how we brew each one. There are rules to be followed for the appropriate grinding and weighing, water use, dosing, tamping, and extraction ratios, among other requirements. Our specifications are unique to **joe,** just as every coffee bar has its own methods of brewing its signature coffees. Here we share some of the factors that the **joe** barista learns and executes to create the coffees so loved by our customers.

WATER: In New York City, we are lucky to drink tap water that has been rated among the best in the United States; however, coffee bars in other areas of the country will often add water softener as well as additional filtering systems to their water supply. At **joe** the great New York tap water that flows to our brewing equipment passes through a sediment and a carbon filter, which not only assist in reducing any chlorine taste and odor that might be there, but also prevent scale buildup on the interior of the machine.

COFFEE: For our drip machines, those that brew our house, single origin, and decaffeinated coffees, we use freshly ground beans. The blend that we favor for the **joe** house blend is one that we like to call "accessible"—that is, a blend that creates an easy-to-drink, everyday delicious cup that is sweet and clean on the palate. We have had many different blends over the years, and they have all been delicious and easy to drink. At

this writing, Gabby is loving our Costa Rica Finca La Clara. It has a great balance of sweetness and fruit along with a light roast profile that she finds rewarding. The **joe** blend changes seasonally and may also change within three weeks to two months of introduction, depending on inventory and seasonal preference.

For espresso, the beans are seven to ten days off roast. This is because espresso is brewed at such high pressure that fresh beans are just too volatile, allowing the natural gases in the coffee to be prominent once brewed. For espresso, the ideal blend should be well balanced and extremely low in acidity, giving a complex experience over the entire palate. We start with a base component (usually Brazilian beans) that creates the backdrop for the mid- or high component (origins selected by season and taste) that is added for accent and acidity. When buying coffee for home use, we recommend that you ask your local baristas what their system for blending might be and what optimal time window for usage they recommend for brewing their blend at home.

We look for similar characteristics (sweet, clean, balanced) in both our house blend and our espresso, while our ever-changing single origin coffees give **joe** fans the opportunity to experience a more adventuresome taste on a daily basis. For the latter, coffee can be less approachable and thus more daring.

GRINDERS: For espresso preparation at **joe**, we use a Mazzer Robur E espresso grinder, a programmable electronic dosing grinder. It is a conical burr grinder that shears the beans, producing almost microscopic flake-like coffee granules that have the most surface area allowing for maximum extraction during brewing. In contrast to a burr grinder, a blade grinder chops the coffee into irregular granules, which results in uneven extraction. Also, since water is lazy, it will simply go around the more rock-shaped granules created by the blade grinder and, consequently, will not fully extract the flavor.

Our grinder is efficient because we can set it to dose a specific amount of coffee every time and still allow for adjustments to be made to give exact and reproducible amounts throughout the day and to address varying environmental concerns. Its speed is a tremendous aid to the busy barista who, with the simple push of a button, can move the preferred dose of perfectly ground coffee right into the espresso machine's portafilter. This is important because all espresso coffee is made with beans that are ground per shot.

Because espresso is such a volatile ingredient—reacting to differences in air temperature, burr temperature, humidity, the amount of people in the room, the commingling of air-conditioning and outside air, and so forth—it is important that a barista understand the necessity of grind adjustment. A truly great barista will change the grind dozens of times a day, making small, precise adjustments to ensure that the brewed cup is perfect.

COFFEE FACTS:

The residents of Finland drink the most coffee per capita in the world. Although the United States is the largest importer of beans, Americans use an average of eleven pounds a year while Finns use an average of twenty-four pounds.

SCALE: After experimenting with a variety of scales, we now use just a high-quality digital home kitchen scale that precisely measures in grams. There are many brands on the market, and most are priced under fifty dollars. Depending upon the blend, day, age, and other variables found in freshly roasted beans, the amount of coffee needed to pull one double shot of espresso usually ranges from seventeen to twenty-one grams. In coffee parlance, the amount of coffee used is called a dose, and the precise amount is only discovered after trial and error and many, many tastings of each blend. Different beans have

different densities, so sometimes a heavier dose may enhance the lower notes in the coffee as it is these low notes that are found in the denser beans. Even after the exact weight is determined, our baristas pull and taste shots at the beginning of each shift and on an hourly basis to ensure that the espresso is as desired.

MACHINES: Our house, single origin, and decaffeinated coffees are brewed in large Fetco drip brand machines that give us the ability to program the specifics of our signature clean, sweet flavor. Their efficiency creates a coffee that is almost comparable to our manual pour-overs. (See page 119 for directions to create a manual pour-over at home just as we do at **joe.**) Coffee beans are ground just before brewing, just as we would do for any coffee. This automated system is preprogrammed with the water-to-coffee ratio, and it is not often necessary to change it. The coffee is brewed

directly into thermal carafes and is, as far as we are concerned, the finest way to brew and serve large batches of coffee.

For espresso, we use La Marzocco GB5 espresso machines, which we, along with many others, consider the top of the line. It is a dual boiler machine, having one for brewing coffee and one for creating steam, and it allows the barista to pull a shot and steam milk simultaneously. The ground coffee is placed in a portafilter and is tamped down using a metal tamper. Water temperature is perhaps the most important element in creating the perfect espresso shot, and this machine gives the barista the ability to set the extraction temperature to his liking. At **joe** we pull our shots at about 200°F, give or take a degree or two depending upon the particular espresso blend. To make the perfect espresso, it is essential that correctly tamped ground beans and desired water temperature are met with exact timing. At **joe** we generally tamp down seventeen to twenty-one grams using a concentrated amount of water, resulting in an extraordinarily flavorful and rich brew that measures in at between 1.75 and 2 ounces.

EXTRACTION: The extraction time varies depending upon the blend, the volatility of the coffee, and many environmental factors. It will generally range from twenty-two to twenty-seven seconds, but at the end of the day, it simply comes down to how the coffee tastes. The barista uses his or her skill to set the appropriate extraction time to create the perfect cup. Overextracted espresso will tend to have more yellow hues and a sharp, bitter flavor, and while underextracted espresso might be pleasing on the palate, it will be shorter in volume and lack the complexity of a fully realized shot.

PULLING THE PERFECT SHOT

Day after day, Amanda Byron and her team put baristas-to-be through session after session of espresso and milk training in our training lab. There is a bit of chemistry to learn, as it is the intense pressure created by the machine that emulsifies the oils in the coffee and brings about the microscopic bubbles (gas droplets) that produce the crema, the creamy foam-like topping.

Learning how to pull the perfect shot takes hours of practice, as does learning to steam the milk required to make milk-based espresso drinks. The goal is to get the dosing, distributing, and tamping as consistent as possible so that there is complete control of the drink. The only thing that should change on a daily basis is the grind, which is dictated by environmental factors. The end result should be a tiny cup filled with very sweet but complex flavors, a potent scent, a balanced taste, and a pleasing mouth-feel that lingers for a few minutes.

First the shot glass or demitasse cup is warmed, and then the following steps take place:

1 Activate the grinder.

2 Remove the portafilter from the grouphead and lightly knock out the used espresso cake (the puck).

3 Wipe the portafilter with a clean, dry cloth.

4 Dose the espresso into your portafilter.

Note: After dosing, you may choose to lightly tap the portafilter on the forks of the grinder to settle the grounds a bit. We do this step when we feel it is needed for a particular blend or a particular kind of extraction.

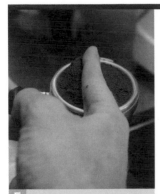

5 Begin your distribution by using your finger to push the grinds around until they rest evenly in the basket. There are many distribution techniques, but the most important element is that your distribution be consistent every time.

6 Holding the tamper evenly between your thumb and forefinger and with your forearm perpendicular to the counter, press down on the espresso with about twenty pounds of pressure.

7 It is important that the tamper be even so that the espresso cake is as level as possible.

8 Twist the tamper to release it from the coffee, taking care not to press down further as you twist.

9 The actual weight is not the important factor; it is that you be consistent from shot to shot.

10 Clean off the edges of the portafilter.

11 Activate the grouphead for about three seconds to release any coffee that might have been stuck to the screen and to bring the grouphead back up to brew temperature.

12 Insert the portafilter into the grouphead.

13 Pull the shot.

Turn off the pump when all of the essential flavors have been extracted from the shot.

Serve the shot.

COFFEE FACTS:

The first espresso machine was made in France in 1822.

The fundamentals of steaming milk are also a necessary skill set for a barista.

When milk is properly steamed, it should have a thick, velvetlike consistency with the appearance of wet paint. The tiny bubbles that form the foam are referred to as micro-bubbles; large bubbles are undesirable since they diminish the full-flavor experience of properly foamed foam, and they create an unappealing, loose foam from which you cannot create latte art. At **joe,** we steam milk to order just as we grind coffee to order. Any extra is tossed, and milk is never resteamed.

Here are the steps for steaming milk for a twelve-ounce latte:

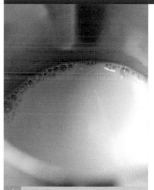  

1 Fill a twenty-ounce milk-steaming pitcher to about three-quarters of an inch below the bottom of the pour spout.

2 Submerge the tip of the steam wand about a half inch into the milk. (If the wand is too close to the top of the milk, the milk will splash out, and if it is too far down, no air will be introduced.)

3 Turn the steam wand on full-force.

Immediately take your right hand and place it under the pitcher so that the increase in heat can be felt. We gently pat the pitcher throughout the steaming process because if you leave your hand on the pitcher, it will come up to temperature as the milk does and you will get an inaccurate reading of when the milk is at its optimal temperature.

4

Stretch the milk until it reaches about 100°F—about seven seconds will elapse. (This is done mostly by ear and takes some experience—the milk will hiss slightly a few times when the steam wand touches the surface of the milk, indicating that air is being properly introduced. If the milk makes especially loud noises, as if it were screaming, more air needs to be introduced.)

5

At this point, submerge the wand completely and move it to the side of the pitcher to achieve the necessary whirlpooling effect that creates the desired micro-bubbles.

6

Turn off the steam when the bottom of the pitcher is hot to the touch (about 150°F), taking care not to bring the tip of the wand out of the milk until the steam is completely off.

7

Swirl the milk until ready to pour into the espresso. The pitcher may also be banged on the counter to release any large bubbles.

8 Pour the milk into the drink and serve.

COFFEE FACTS:

The popular "latte" is primarily an American phenomenon. If you ask for a latte in Italy, you will be served a glass of milk.

When steaming milk for cappuccino, the process is similar to steaming for a latte, except that the experience is stretched out. A **joe** cappuccino is much lighter in weight and foamier than a latte. The appearance of the milk remains a beautiful, velvety micro-bubble with the wet paint sheen, but it has a thicker texture on the palate. This is because the initial steaming phase is longer with an increased amount of air introduced into the milk.

Many of our regular customers still get excited when they see the artwork in their espresso drinks. Called latte art, the design is only possible when the pulled shot and the steamed milk are executed in an exceptional manner. Although we can give you the basic steps, there is no practical way to teach the process. In order for the art to be accomplished, all motion must be as smooth and fluid as possible, and this only comes with lots and lots of practice. At **joe** every latte presented to a customer must have a design on it. And many of our baristas have become masters of the art, creating original designs that more than "wow" our fans.

Here are the basic steps:

1 Tip the cup that holds the espresso, angling it toward the milk pitcher.

2 Very slowly, begin pouring the milk into the cup, starting with the stream hitting the wall of the cup closest to the spout. The stream should be about the thickness of a pencil.

3 Carefully observe how the milk rather slides underneath the crema on the espresso—this is why the cup must be tipped. Poured into an untipped cup, the milk will break the crema and give the barista less "canvas" on which to execute the art.

The difficult steps:

4. Continue to pour in a slow, steady stream, moving the pitcher toward the center of the cup *or* aiming for the opposite side of the cup.

5. At this point, a "halo" should form around where the pour stream comes in contact with the espresso.

6. When you see this halo, increase the speed of the pour by about double. The stream should now be about the size of a thin straw.

7. When the cup is half full and the "halo" has formed, the difficult steps begin as the movement of the milk must be carefully controlled to create the basic "rosetta" (a delicate fern leaf design that forms as the hot, foamy milk pushes up to the surface) that is the keystone of the art.

8. We tend to refer to the action as a wiggle, but it more resembles a pumping action—like engaging a bike brake. It is important to visualize that you are folding your steamed milk into the crema of the espresso rather than "drawing" a picture on top.

9. As you increase your wiggle, start to pull the pitcher back toward the original start point, maintaining a slow, steady stream as you move.

10. At this point, the rosetta leaves begin to open up at the bottom and taper off as the pitcher is retracted.

11. When the cup is almost full and the milk pitcher is almost empty, the pitcher should be back at the beginning point at the far edge of the cup.

12. Rather than pulling the stream up and out, push it back through the petals of the rosetta, creating the stem. This is called the "pull-through," and it can go right over the far edge of the cup.

Being a great barista takes an enormous amount of time, skill, and talent. One way that many of our **joe** baristas stay in shape is through participation in international competitions and local events called "throwdowns" or "brew-downs." A win in an international competition is exceedingly prestigious and can lead to a high-powered career in the specialty coffee business. On the other hand, the local events, although competitive, are also meant to be occasions when coffee fanatics can gather after hours, drink beer, and spur each other on to wildly adventuresome latte art. The rules are quite simple: a specific time (usually one minute) to pull a shot, steam milk, and create a stunning rosetta. For a trained barista this is all second nature, but it is not so easy to do after a day at the espresso machine, lots of caffeine, and a couple of beers! The judges are usually fellow baristas who rate each latte for its execution of design. Sometimes, but not always, the winner goes home with a cash prize or, at the least, a few pounds of coffee. Although throwdowns are real contests with the winners gaining a degree of specialty coffee notoriety, in actual fact they give baristas a chance to gather, relax, have some fun, and share the latest coffee gossip. This is the ultimate mingling of coffee and popular culture. And, at **joe** we are constantly celebrating the championships of our many superb baristas.

BRINGING it HOME

In the specialty coffee business, we have found that most of our customers don't just have a cup of coffee to wake up and jump-start their day. Instead, they are looking for the finest, most flavorful cup of coffee available based on taste, not its caffeinated properties. They are willing to take classes in all aspects of coffee growing, tasting, and brewing. They are willing to pay the premium price required for seasonality, Direct Trade, and expeditious roasting and delivery. All of this translates to their home brew, as we find the sale of whole beans and grinding and brewing equipment to be rapidly growing. Some consumers now even *buy* green beans that they can roast at home, a process that, unbelievably, was once commonplace in the home kitchen. But that is now considered the height of coffee geekdom.

At **joe** all of our beans are packed in one-way valve bags printed with the roast date to ensure freshness for the home brew. Sealed, freshly roasted beans emit carbon dioxide that must escape to keep the beans' natural flavor intact; the valve allows this to occur. Once opened, we recommend that the bag be tightly sealed and stored, preferably in an airtight container in a cool, dark spot, for no more than two weeks. Although we can grind a bag of beans to order, we think it best if the consumer grinds just enough for each cup to be made right before brewing. Ground beans, even properly sealed, only have a few hours before losing their fresh flavor.

Dedicated coffee lovers are willing to spend large sums of money to acquire the best home brewing equipment, including fine espresso machines, grinders, and brewers. At the opposite end of the spectrum, we can recommend one of the oldest and simplest brewing methods, using hot water poured over ground coffee. This method will easily produce an excellent cup of coffee in the home kitchen.

For all intents and purposes, there are two procedures used to brew coffee—the immersion method and the drip method. With the immersion method, ground coffee is totally covered with water (usually hot) and allowed to steep, while with the drip method, ground coffee is placed in a filter and hot water is poured over it, allowing the water to slowly drip down into a pot. Other interesting methods include the Japanese cold drip and, of course, the old-fashioned and now rarely used percolator.

With today's growing interest in specialty coffees, the Internet has been a great

resource for a coffee enthusiast to explore the world of home brewing, particularly espresso making. A great many websites and blogs are devoted exclusively to the art of coffee, featuring reports and conversations about beans, brewing methods, and equipment. They are great places to gather information if you are new to the world of specialty coffee and are excellent sources for reviews and user endorsements as you prepare to purchase what can be an expensive home espresso machine.

In this chapter, you will find all of the requirements and equipment we suggest for successful home brewing. All of the methods that we discuss will require freshly roasted beans, a fine quality grinder, a scale, a kettle, filtered water, a timer, and simple cups that have been preheated from which you can enjoy your home brew. Of course, it should go without saying that all of the equipment should be absolutely clean with no soap or old coffee residue.

If you have, like we do in New York City, superb tap water that will infuse no undesirable taste or odor into your coffee, you can use it to make your brew. Just

remember that *if* you can taste the water in your brewed coffee, you will need to change to bottled spring or filtered water.

For superb home-brewed coffee, just as in a specialty coffee bar, the most important elements are the quality of the coffee and the water. The other elements are also important, with the quality of the grinder being a significant contributor to excellent home-brewed coffee. A number of grinders can be found on the market, but we can only recommend a burr grinder. You don't want to use a small, inexpensive (around twenty dollars) blade-style or propeller grinder, which chops the beans and produces an inconsistent grind as well as heats the beans through the speed of the rapidly turning blades. Instead, get a burr grinder, which uses two revolving metal wheels or conical grinding elements that shear the beans. The result is small particles of coffee with a larger amount of surface area allowing maximum extraction of flavor. Burr grinders can be either mechanical or manual, although mechanical is more efficient. Most burr grinders that we endorse, such as the Baratza, Rancilio Rocky, or Solis Maestro Plus, cost in the hundreds of dollars, but you can find quality burr grinders for less than two hundred dollars.

Each type of brewed coffee will require a specific type of grind. For instance, a French press demands a coarse grind, about the size of large sea salt crystals. Drip machines and Chemex will use a medium grind, about the size of kosher salt crystals. Single cup drippers like Hario V60 will use a slighty finer grind, and finally espresso machines require a very fine, almost powdery grind. It is a basic rule that the longer the coffee is going to be in contact with the water, the coarser the grind. At **joe** we recommend about two tablespoons of ground coffee for every six ounces of water. However, we have found that weighing the coffee and the water results in a more accurate and precise cup. In that case, for a 12-ounce cup of coffee we use about 21–24 grams of coffee per 340 grams of water.

All of the recommended home brewing methods require that the hot drink be consumed immediately—or, at most, within ten to fifteen minutes—after being brewed. With some methods, there is no way to keep the liquid hot and fresh in the brewing container, and with other methods, the coffee will be overextracted and bitter when the coffee and water are left to commingle for more than fifteen to twenty minutes.

Following is a brief explanation of the various methods available to brew a perfect cup of coffee at home.

BREWING METHODS

CHEMEX

One of the simplest and best-known home brewing methods is done through the use of an hourglass-shaped Chemex coffee carafe. A beautifully designed, laboratory-like vessel, the Chemex was invented in the 1930s by a German scientist who was

clearly interested in creating a kitchen classic that echoed the modernist creed of beauty combined with straightforward functionality. It is inexpensive and very easy to use. The original Chemex has a wooden collar around the mid-section, but there is now a version that features a simple glass handle. It comes in a variety of sizes ranging from three to ten cups.

In addition to the standard requirements listed on page 108, you will only need the carafe and authorized Chemex filters to use the Chemex.

1. Fill a kettle with cold water and place over high heat. While the water is coming to a boil (this should take about five minutes), prepare your coffee.

2. Weigh the coffee following the above recommendation. A good starting point is 52 grams of coffee for 740 grams (or 26 ounces) of water.

3. Grind the coffee to a medium grind, about the size of kosher salt.

4. By now, your water should have come to a boil. Remove the kettle from the heat and let stand for about ten seconds, noting that you want to use water that is 195°F to 205°F to prepare your coffee.

5. Place the Chemex filter into position in the top half of the carafe, pulling the filter apart and lightly pressing three sides against the pour spout and the remaining side against the opposing side. (The instructions are on the Chemex filter box.)

6. Carefully pour a small amount of hot water around and through the filter to eliminate any contaminant tastes it might hold and to preheat the Chemex carafe.

7. Pour out and discard the water used to dampen the filter. The filter will not fall out of position.

8. Place the ground coffee into the filter.

9. Place the carafe on the scale, making sure that the scale has been tared to zero.

10. Pouring in concentric circles, slowly pour one hundred grams of water over the grounds to saturate.

11. Allow the coffee to "bloom" (you will see the grinds puff up and air escape through small holes) for about one minute. The bloom allows the fresh coffee to degas just a bit and evenly saturate all of the grounds before you add the rest of the water.

12. Immediately and carefully begin pouring the prescribed amount of water in concentric circles over the dampened grounds, pausing your pour when the height of the coffee reaches about an inch from the top of the filter.

13. When the coffee finishes dripping through, which should take about four minutes, remove the filter (which, including the wet coffee grounds, is a great addition to the compost heap) and enjoy!

CAFE SOLO

This total immersion coffee brewer is made by a Danish company, Eva Denmark, that has won many awards for its design sensibility. With this particular coffeemaker, not only does the design sing, but the coffee brewed is spectacular. Introduced in 2003, Cafe Solo has not yet received wide home use, but we can recommend it without reservation.

The brewing pack (which, by the way, comes in an equally well-designed box) is composed of a forty-ounce glass carafe, a neoprene cover, a filter, a no-drip lid, and a stirring spoon. The zipped-up, jacket-like cover ensures that the brewed coffee remains hot for up to thirty minutes (even though we recommend it being held no more than fifteen minutes); the filter keeps the grounds from leeching into the poured coffee; the layered lid opens automatically and allows a drip-free pour; and the spoon is used both to mix the grounds into the water and aerate them, allowing any air trapped in the ground coffee to rise to the top.

Cafe Solo

With the immersion method, one of the oldest techniques to brew clean-tasting coffee, it is imperative that you begin with boiling water and a preheated carafe. This is because when the boiling water is poured over the grounds, the temperature immediately drops to about 200°F, the ideal condition for perfect coffee brewing. This temperature extracts about 80 percent of the flavor within the first couple of minutes of brewing. You can brew either the full (thirty-two-ounce) or a half (sixteen-ounce) carafe. Less is not recommended.

1. Boil a kettle of cold water over high heat, and prepare your coffee.

2. Place the jacket onto the Cafe Solo carafe, zipping it about halfway up.

3. Weigh the coffee. For this method, we recommend a starting ratio of 33 grams of coffee for every 525 grams of water.

4. Grind the beans to a coarse grind, about the consistency of coarse sea salt.

5. Pour boiling water into the Cafe Solo carafe to thoroughly heat.

6. Pour out and discard heating water.

7. Pour the freshly ground coffee into the carafe.

8. Set the carafe on the scale, making sure the scale has been tared to zero.

9. Set the timer for four minutes.

10. Immediately begin adding 525 grams of boiling water to the carafe. It should come up to the beginning of the neck of the carafe. The grounds will rise to about an inch from the beginning of the neck, and "bloom" will be observed.

11. After coffee has bloomed for one minute, stir until the ground coffee and water have blended thoroughly, about ten seconds to no more than twenty seconds.

12. Quickly insert the filter funnel into the carafe and immediately place the lid on the filter top.

13. Completely zip up the neoprene jacket.

14. When your timer goes off, begin gently pouring into preheated cups by tilting the carafe upward to about forty-five degrees and turning your wrist slowly as you pour. This will allow the coffee to be evenly extracted. To create the perfect cup of coffee, the entire carafe should be decanted in one pour so that the brew is not overly agitated or overextracted.

FRENCH PRESS
ALSO KNOWN AS A "PLUNGER POT" OR "COFFEE PRESS"

First developed in the late 1800s, the French press is a very simple method of steeping coffee grounds in water for a few minutes and then pushing a fine mesh plunger down into the water, separating the grounds from the now brewed coffee. Because the coffee does not pass through a paper or other filter, the resultant brew is generally a bit larger in body and lends itself well to full-bodied, earthy coffees. Tea is often brewed in a French press, also.

The device has undergone many modifications since its invention. Contemporary French presses are usually composed of a cylindrical pot made of clear glass (although often now plastic) that is fitted with a lid and metal plunger. The plunger fits snuggly into the cylinder. The lid is centered around a rod on which the fine mesh (either metal or nylon) plunger is also centered.

When using a French press, it is imperative that you begin with boiling water. Coffee brewed with a French press has more body and is more strongly flavored than coffee prepared through the drip method; therefore it should be poured as soon as it is brewed to prevent overextraction and bitterness.

1. Boil a kettle of cold water, and prepare your coffee.

2. Weigh the coffee. For this method, we recommend a starting ratio of 33 grams of coffee for every 525 grams of water.

3. Grind the desired amount of beans to a coarse grind (a bit larger than a grain of kosher salt). Coffee that has been too finely ground will clog the mesh and cause extreme pressure to build when you push the plunger.

4. By now, your water should have come to a boil. Remove the kettle from the heat and let stand for about ten seconds; you want to use water that is 195°F to 205°F.

5. Place the French press cylinder on a dry, flat, heat-proof surface and carefully remove the plunger.

6. Place the weighed ground coffee into the pot.

7. Carefully pour the hot water into the pot, leaving an inch of space at the top. On a typical French press this will be just to the top of the metal band.

8. Gently stir the grounds into the water. This step allows the grounds to mingle and settle into the bottom of the pot.

9. Return the plunger unit to the pot, placing it carefully on top of the cylinder. The mesh sieve should be at the top of the pot and the rod should be sticking completely up through the lid.

10. Allow the coffee to brew for four minutes.

11. Holding onto the pot handle and using gentle weight, carefully apply pressure to the top of the rod to begin pushing the plunger down into the hot liquid. It is important that you do not put excess pressure on the plunger or wiggle it around. It should slowly and evenly depress downward because if the rod is crooked, grounds will leak into the liquid. This gentle approach will produce the most flavorful coffee. In addition, excessive force can cause the hot liquid to spurt out of the pot, possibly burning you.

12. If your pot has a pour spout, turn the lid to open.

13. Slowly pour the coffee into heated cups.

14. Do not let the brewed coffee stay in the pot after pressing as it will continue to brew. If not serving immediately, pour the coffee into a heated thermos.

POUR OVER

For this method you need little equipment. At its simplest, all that is required is a ceramic cone lined with a paper filter placed over a heated coffee cup. It can, of course, be used to make coffee in a carafe. At **joe** we use the Hario V60 cone for speed of service and ease of use, but there are other ceramic drippers, such as the beehive or the Bonmac, which are also very good. The Hario V60 is a single-cup coffee dripper with a large open base that allows for even flow.

1. Prepare your coffee while boiling a kettle of cold water.

2. Grind the desired amount of beans to a medium-fine drip grind (about the size of a grain of kosher salt).

3. Weigh the ground coffee. For a 12-ounce cup, we usually begin with a ratio of 21 to 24 grams of coffee for 340 grams of water.

4. By now, your water should have come to a boil. Remove the kettle from the heat and let stand for about ten seconds; the water should be 195°F to 205°F.

5. Gently place the filter in the cone and put the cone on top of the cup.

6. Carefully pour a small amount of hot water around and through the filter to eliminate any contaminant tastes it might hold and to preheat the container.

7. Pour out and discard the water used to dampen the filter.

8. Place the ground coffee into the filter.

9. Place the carafe or cup on the scale, making sure that the scale has been tared to zero.

10. Carefully and slowly pour about fifty grams of water (that is ten seconds off the boil) over the grounds to saturate. The weight of water should be about twice your weight in coffee, so about forty-five to fifty grams of water.

11. Allow the coffee to bloom for thirty seconds to one minute, depending upon the freshness of the coffee.

12. After the bloom, continue carefully pouring water in 100-gram intervals in small concentric circles, never allowing the coffee to reach about an inch below the top of the filter.

13. Once you have added the desired weight of water, let the brew finish, discard the grounds and enjoy.

OTHER HOME BREWERS

AeroPress is, in theory, similar to a French press in that water and coffee are mixed together for a brief period and then a filter and plunger system is used to create the brew. A simple plastic pump that sits directly on a single cup, AeroPress is primarily used to brew a single cup of espresso; however, you can brew up to four cups. To make "American" coffee, you simply add a half cup of hot water to the espresso. Many feel that it is the simplest and best device for making a quick, smooth, rich espresso at home.

Yama Tabletop Syphon Brewer is a Japanese glass coffeemaker that is a modern version of an older siphon system of brewing. From its name, you will note that it is not brewed on a stovetop. The bottom receptacle is placed on a counter or tabletop and filled with hot water, which is further heated by an alcohol burner that sits underneath it. The coffee grounds are placed in the top receptacle, and the pressure of the heat causes the water to rise and steep the coffee grounds. Once all of the water has risen to the top, the burner is removed, and the brewed coffee then drips back into the bottom receptacle. Many people feel that this system gives the brewer more control over the outcome and creates a brewed coffee that is extremely clean with defined flavor and aroma.

COFFEE FACTS:

The brand name Sanka, one of the earliest decaffeinated coffees to be marketed in the United States, comes from the French *sans* (without) *caffeine* (caffeine). It had its greatest impact in the commercial world as a sponsor of the wildly popular *I Love Lucy* television show.

HOME ESPRESSO MACHINES

Espresso is essentially coffee brewed under high pressure, and making it is simply another method of brewing coffee. There are many types of espresso machines made for home use; some are quite simple, while others can compete almost one on one with commercial machines. Although many small appliance manufacturers make a steam-run home espresso machine, most of them do not have the pressure capacity or temperature stability to create great espresso.

When purchasing a home espresso machine, you will want to look at its consistency in preparing the cup you desire. The machine should also hold the same temperature and pressure, never compromising the quality of the shot. In addition, it is helpful if the machine can be programmed to adjust the extraction pressure and water temperature should you wish to change these parameters. The machine should be user-friendly and compatible with your kitchen space. While barista technique stays relatively the same regardless of equipment, each manufacturer has its own instructions to use its particular machine and those should be followed.

An espresso machine is a comparatively simple device used to easily heat water to a desired temperature and push it through a specified amount of tamped-down ground coffee (a puck) to create a rich cup of coffee. The method by which this occurs defines the type of machine. There are essentially two types of machines made for home use: manual or automatic with each type having subcategories. Manual machines are

either spring piston lever or direct lever, and automatic machines are semi-automatic, automatic, or super-automatic. In addition, the semi-automatic and automatic machines also have subcategories. A brief description of each type follows.

Manual

The power on these machines, also known as lever espresso machines, comes via hand pressure on a lever, either a spring piston lever or a direct lever. They were the first home machines (although they are used in many Italian coffee bars) to produce quality espresso through pressure rather than with steam. Spring piston machines have an internal spring device that has been calibrated to force water through ground

COFFEE FACTS:

In 1901 in Chicago, a Japanese-American chemist named Satori Kato invented just-add-hot-water instant coffee.

coffee at a defined pressure. The brewer manually presses the lever to initiate the spring's action, while letting go of the lever allows the spring to begin the process of forcing the water through the grounds. With a direct lever machine, it is the brewer who does the actual pressing of the lever with no help from any internal device. Although they are both capable of creating a delicious espresso, it is the hands-on skill that produces either a great cup or a barely drinkable one.

Automatic Machines

There are three major categories of semi- and fully automated machines. These are 1) the single boiler, dual-use, which has two separate thermometers for heating water and for heating milk but cannot brew coffee and steam milk at the same time; 2) single boiler, heat exchange, which has a large boiler capable of maintaining the desired steam-creating 240°F water temperature and can brew and steam milk simultaneously; and 3) the dual boiler, which has two separate boilers, one to maintain the appropriate temperature for brewing water and one for steam, and can also brew and steam milk at the same time. The first category can cost under one thousand dollars while the other two range from one thousand dollars to well over that price. For example, La Marzocco, whose commercial machines are used at all **joe** coffee bars, makes a home espresso machine that retails for about $6,500. You will pay a premium for a high-quality, long-lasting machine, but if you are a serious coffee drinker, the investment is well worth making.

Semi-Automatic Machines

With a semi-automatic machine, much of the process is automated, including the activation; however, it is the brewer's decision when to manually switch the pump on and off.

Automatic Machines

With a fully automated machine, all systems are automated, either through presetting or programming; all the brewer has to do is push a button to activate the process and then the machine turns off automatically.

Super-Automatic Machines

A super-automatic machine does everything from grinding to ejecting the used grounds (the puck) with the press of a button. Specialty coffee brewers do not recommend them, as the barista has little control over the quality of the grinding, the degree of tamping, and so forth.

MOKA POT OR STOVETOP ESPRESSO COFFEEMAKER:

This device was invented in Italy in the mid-1900s by Alfonso Bialetti to bring the familiar coffee bar espresso into the home. The moka pot, a three-chambered, steam-based stovetop espresso maker, was the foundation for the growth of the Bialetti company, now one of Italy's largest coffee machine and kitchen-ware companies. The classic three-chamber design has won many international awards, influenced many industrial designers, and remained constant for decades. A number of fine moka pots are available on the market, ranging in price from twenty dollars to more than two hundred dollars.

MYPRESSI TWIST

This is a small handheld espresso maker that uses innovative pneumatic technology to allow the home brewer to create an excellent espresso without an expensive machine. The apparatus can create either two single espressos or one double. It requires gas cartridges and will work with either coffee pods or your own ground beans. It can be used anywhere as long as you have the cartridges and coffee.

COFFEE FACTS:

It is said that the Maxwell House coffee slogan—"good to the last drop"—came about in 1907 after President Theodore Roosevelt proclaimed it so when he served a cup.

ACIDITY: The measurement of bright flavors in a coffee.

AGED COFFEE: Coffee beans held in their green form for an extended period of time.

AMERICANO: Espresso diluted with hot water.

ARABICA: The main species of coffee bean used in specialty coffees.

BARISTA: The skilled artisan who prepares all coffee drinks at a coffee bar.

BLEND: A specific mixture of beans from different origins for the purpose of creating a flavor profile.

BODY: The feel of the weight of brewed coffee in the mouth.

BURR GRINDER OR MILL: An electric coffee grinder with two shredding burrs (or disks) that is the most precise method of grinding coffee beans.

CAFÉ AU LAIT: Traditionally a French breakfast coffee drink made of coffee and hot milk.

CAFESOLO: A single immersion coffee brewer (see page 113).

CAPPUCCINO: Espresso combined with steamed milk to total a five- to seven-ounce drink.

CARAMELIZATION: The sweet flavors brought out during roasting of the coffee bean.

CHEMEX: An hourglass-shaped glass filter drip coffee pot (see page 110).

CHERRY: The name used to describe the fruit in which the coffee bean is a seed.

CLEAN CUP: Cupper's term for a coffee that appears to be defect-free.

CLEVER COFFEE DRIPPER: A filter cone with a stopper that allows coffee to steep before dripping.

CLOVER: A single-cup brewing machine that, some say, brews exceptionally flavorful coffee. The Coffee Equipment Company invented the Clover in Seattle in 2003. The company is now owned by Starbucks, and the machines will be exclusively used in Starbucks stores. Some machines are still in operation in small coffee bars across the United States.

COLD BREW COFFEE: Coffee prepared by allowing the grounds to steep for twelve to twenty-four hours in cold water, with the resultant strong brew diluted with milk or used to make iced coffee. The devices used to make cold brew coffee range from steeping in buckets to elaborate multi-chambered commercially manufactured glass towers. Also known as cold drip.

CORTADO: From the Spanish word for *cut*, espresso combined with steamed milk in a drink yielding about five ounces. Also called a Gibraltar.

CREMA: The rich, oily, foam-like topping on espresso, consisting of the tiny bubbles created by the pressure of the espresso machine.

CUP OF EXCELLENCE: An annual international competition to name the best coffee grown by specific regions (see page 10).

CUPPING: Professional means of tasting and evaluating coffee (see pages 30 and 38).

DIRECT METHOD: A method of removing caffeine from green coffee beans not used in the world of specialty coffee.

DIRECT TRADE: The method by which green coffee is purchased directly from the farmer (see page 13).

DOPPIO: A double shot of espresso; a term rarely used in the United States.

DOSE: The specific amount of coffee ratio to water used to brew coffee or espresso.

DRIP COFFEE: Coffee brewed through a filter, whereby hot water is poured over ground coffee.

DRY PROCESS: Natural process of drying coffee cherries in the sun before removing the bean.

ESPRESSO: A one- to two-ounce strong, rich, flavorful coffee made under pressure by forcing hot water through finely ground coffee.

EXTRACTION: The method by which flavor is distilled from ground coffee.

FAIR TRADE: A method of coffee buying whereby the grower is guaranteed a specified price for the beans. For more information, visit www.transfairusa.org.

FILTER: A triangular-shaped paper or a plastic, glass, gold-colored, or ceramic cone-shaped device used to hold coffee grounds when making drip coffee. The latter may or may not be lined with a paper filter.

FILTER COFFEE: Coffee made through hot water being poured over coffee grounds placed in a filter.

FILTER HOLDER: See portafilter.

FLANNEL DRIP: Coffee made in a woodneck Japanese brewer that uses flannel filters, which must be hand-washed and refrigerated between uses. Also known as a nel-drip.

FRENCH PRESS: A glass or metal container with a plunger and mesh filter in which coffee is produced by steeping the grounds in hot water and then plunging them to the bottom of the pot. Also known as a press pot (see page 116).

GREEN BEANS: Unroasted coffee beans.

HARIO KETTLE: A stainless steel kettle imported from Japan with a long, thin, swan-like spout used to pour a thin, steady stream of hot water over coffee grounds. Also known as a Buono kettle.

INDIRECT METHOD: Method of removing caffeine from specialty coffee beans (see page 20).

LATTE: Espresso blended with steamed milk to total eight- to twelve-ounce drink.

LATTE ART: The design seen on the top of a latte, created by a skilled barista. It is created by folding perfectly steamed milk into the crema of espresso.

MACCHIATO: Espresso "marked" with steamed milk to total a two- to three-ounce drink; technically called an espresso macchiato.

MICRO-LOT: Coffee beans from a single origin or from a specific section of a particular farm or plantation.

MOCHA: Espresso combined with chocolate syrup and hot steamed milk.

MONSOONING: A method of processing coffee in which the beans are subjected to the harsh, unpredictable monsoon season in Indonesia.

PORTAFILTER: The filter and handle on an espresso machine that is packed with coffee.

POUR-OVER: Coffee made by slowly pouring water in a gentle stream over a filter cone.

PROPELLER GRINDER: Small, inexpensive electric grinder with blades used to grind coffee beans.

PUCK: The tight cylinder of espresso in a portafilter.

PULL: The term used to describe making an espresso, relating back to when espresso was made by manually pulling on a lever.

REDEYE: Brewed coffee with espresso, also called Black Eye or Shot in the Dark.

RESERVOIR: The water-holding chamber on an espresso machine.

RISTRETTO: A short, concentrated espresso; it means "restricted pour."

ROAST: The process of taking green beans to a specific degree of heat to develop the inherent flavors.

ROAST DATE: The date printed on a bag of specialty coffee beans designating when roasting occurred and signifying the length of time that the coffee should be held before use.

ROASTER: The machine or the person that roasts green coffee beans.

SEASONALITY: The designated period of time that a specific coffee should be in the market based on when it was harvested.

SILVERSKIN: The paper-like coating on a green coffee bean.

SINGLE ORIGIN: Coffee from a specific place—either a farm or a particular area of a farm or, sometimes, even a country, depending upon how a country separates its lots.

SIPHON: A complicated, multi-device, vacuum pressure coffeemaker that produces coffee with pure flavor and exceptional clarity. Used only in a few select coffee bars.

SLOW-DRIPPER: A Japanese cold-water coffeemaker consisting of a glass globe and a number of valves and tubes that takes about twelve to eighteen hours to brew a dense coffee often used for iced drinks.

STEAM WAND: The narrow steam pipe on the side of an espresso machine that is used to steam milk.

TAMPER: The flat-bottomed or convex tool used to press ground coffee into the portafilter of an espresso machine or to tamp, the action used to press ground coffee into the metal filter of an espresso machine.

THROWDOWN: A fun-filled gathering where baristas compete for the best presentation of latte art.

WOODNECK: Japanese glass coffeemaker with a flannel filter (see flannel drip).

hese are sources for coffee beans, roasting and brewing equipment, and all other coffee culture paraphernalia.

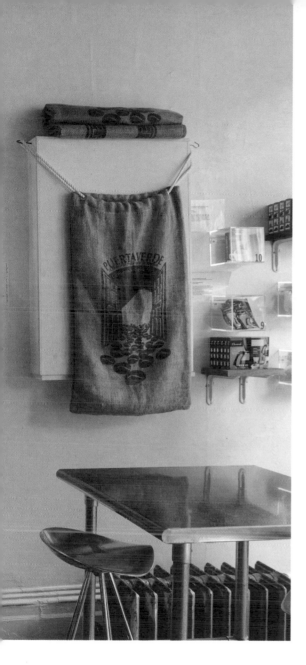

COFFEE BREWING EQUIPMENT AND/OR BEANS

joe
www.joenewyork.com

Intelligentsia
www.intelligentsiacoffee.com

Counter Culture Coffee
www.counterculturecoffee.com

Brew Methods
www.brewmethods.com

Coffeed.com
www.coffeed.com

1st-line Equipment
www.1st-line.com

CoffeeResearch.org
www.coffeeresearch.org

Williams-Sonoma (*for Japanese Coffee Brewing Equipment*)
www.williams-sonoma.com

Espresso Parts
www.espressoparts.com

Roustabout Products
www.roustaboutproducts.com

Chris' Coffee Service
www.chriscoffee.com

Barista Pro Shop
www.baristaproshop.com

HOME BREWING AND ROASTING EQUIPMENT

Mr. Green Beans
www.diycoffeeroasting.com

WOOD-ROASTED COFFEE

Matt's Wood Roasted Organic Coffee
www.mattscoffee.com

Millar's Wood Roasted Coffee
www.millarscoffee.com

PLEASE ORDER
WITH THE
BARISTA

When not in one of our eight **joe** shops, we stop by, sip, and gossip with our fellow coffee enthusiasts in their various coffee bars around the city. Should you be in New York, of course, we'd love to welcome you at any of our **joe** stores, from Grand Central Station to the Brooklyn DeKalb Market. We hope that you will visit us along with some of our favorite coffee bars all across the city. Among them are:

Abraco, 86 East Seventh Street, NYC, 10003, (212) 388-9731

Blue Bottle Coffee, 160 Berry Street, Brooklyn, New York, 11211 (among other locations in New York and California), (718) 387-4160

Café Grumpy, 220 West Twentieth Street, NYC, 10011 (among various locations), (212) 255-5511

Dora, 221 East Broadway, NYC, 10002, (212) 876-8065

Everyman Espresso, 136 East Thirteenth Street, NYC, 10003, (212) 533-0524

Gimme! Coffee, 228 Mott Street, NYC, 10012, (212) 226-4011

Kaffe 1668, 275 Greenwich, #4, NYC, 10007, (212) 693-3750

Ninth Street Espresso, 700 East Ninth Street, NYC, 10009, (212) 358-9225

Oslo Coffee Roasters, 133 Roebling Street, Brooklyn, New York, 11211 (among other locations), (718) 782-0332

RBC, 71 Worth Street, NYC, 10013, (212) 226-1111

Stumptown Coffee Roasters, 18 West Twenty-ninth Street, NYC, 10001, no telephone

Sweetleaf Café, 10-93 Jackson Avenue, Long Island City, New York, 11101, (917) 832-6726

Think Coffee, 248 Mercer Street, NYC, 10012 (among other locations), (212) 228-6226

Third Rail Coffee, 240 Sullivan Street, NYC, 10012, no telephone

There are many superb specialty coffee bars across the United States, and when we travel, we always make sure to put a coffee break on our agenda. Among the really terrific spots where we have personally had the opportunity to sip great coffee are:

Barista, Portland, Oregon

Espresso Vivace, Seattle

Intelligentsia Coffee, Chicago and Los Angeles

Lenox Coffee, Lenox, Massachusetts

Peregrine Espresso, Washington, D.C.

Ritual Coffee Roasters, San Francisco

Stumptown Coffee Roasters, Portland, Oregon, and Seattle

Ultimo Coffee, Philadelphia

Victrola Coffee Roasters, Seattle

RESOURCES

CoffeeGeek; coffeegeek.com.

ECCOCAFFÈ on coffee, Ecco Caffè, www.eccocaffe.com, 2010.

Intelligentsia; www.intelligentsiacoffee.com.

International Coffee Organization, 22 Berners Street, London, W1T 3DD, England; Telephone: +44 (0)20 7612 0600; e-Mail: info@ico.org.

joe Newsletter; www.joenewyork.com.

Kummer, Corby. *The Joy of Coffee: The Essential Guide to Buying, Brewing and Enjoying*. New York: Houghton Mifflin Company, 2003.

Lingle, Ted. *The Coffee Brewing Handbook*. Long Beach, CA: Specialty Coffee Association of America, 1996.

Luttinger, Nina, and Gregory Dicum. *The Coffee Book: Anatomy of an Industry from Crop to the Last Drop*. New York: The New Press, 2006.

Rao, Scott. *The Professional Barista's Handbook: An Expert's Guide to Preparing Espresso, Coffee, and Tea*. Published by author, 2008 (visit www.professional baristashandbook.com to purchase).

Schomer, David C. *Espresso Coffee, Updated: Professional Techniques: How to Identify and Control Each Factor to Perfect Espresso Coffee in a Commercial Espresso Program*. Seattle, WA: Classic Day Publishing, 2004.

Specialty Coffee Association of America; http://scaa.org.

INDEX

ABOUT
the Authors and Photographer

Jonathan and Gabrielle Rubinstein own the small chain of **joe** coffee bars that have been named one of the ten best coffee bars in the United States by *Food and Wine Magazine*, one of the ten outstanding coffee bars in New York City by the *New York Times,* and Best Coffee Bar by *New York Magazine, Time Out,* and *The Village Voice*. The Rubinsteins' radio, television, and media appearances include *The Martha Stewart Show, Martha Stewart Living Radio,* and *Emeril's Table*. Visit them at www .joenewyork.com.

Judith Choate is a multiple James Beard award cookbook author who, besides writing her own books, has written or co-authored many prize-winning books for some of America's greatest chefs.

She lives in New York and celebrates the history and creativity of the American food scene through her blog, www .notesfromjudieskitchen.com.

Steve Pool is an in-demand food photographer who has worked with some of America's leading culinary icons.